WRITING AND ANALYZING EFFECTIVE COMPUTER SYSTEM DOCUMENTATION

WRITING AND ANALYZING EFFECTIVE COMPUTER SYSTEM DOCUMENTATION

Ann Stuart
University of Evansville
Evansville, Indiana

HOLT, RINEHART AND WINSTON
New York Chicago San Francisco Philadelphia
Montreal Toronto London Sydney Tokyo
Mexico City Rio de Janeiro Madrid

Copyright © 1984 CBS College Publishing
All rights reserved.
Address correspondence to:
383 Madison Avenue, New York, NY 10017

Library of Congress Cataloging in Publication Data
Stuart, Ann.
   Writing and analyzing effective computer system documentation.

   Includes index.
   1. Electronic data processing documentation.   I. Title.
QA76.9.D6S78   1984   808'.066001   84-12915
ISBN 0-03-063892-5

Printed in the United States of America

Published simultaneously in Canada

    5 6 7   039   9 8 7 6 5 4 3 2

CBS COLLEGE PUBLISHING
Holt, Rinehart and Winston
The Dryden Press
Saunders College Publishing

Contents

Preface ix

PART ONE
Introduction 1

1. You, Writing and System Documentation 3
Stages and documents of computer system development.

2. A Handbook for the Writer and Critic 6
Analyze the document. Analyze the audience. Organize and outline. Format effectively. Be responsible for what you write. Look at your words. Proofread. Checklist.

3. Structures for Writing 21
Definition. Comparison and contrast. Classification and division. Description. Narration. Process analysis. Procedure. Cause and effect. Persuasion. Checklist.

PART TWO
Analysis 51

4. The Proposal I 53
Definition and function. Writer. Audience. The Talkthrough. Checklist.

5. The Proposal II 57
Problem statement. Solution statement. Operational requirements. Operating environment. Benefits. Budgets and costs. Implementation plan. Evaluation. Alternatives. Checklist.

6. Functional Specification I   90
Definition and function. Writer. Audience. Good work habits. Parts of the functional specification: Title page and table of contents. Problem and solution statement. Assumptions. Glossary. Checklist.

7. Functional Specification II   103
Input and output. Responsibilities. Hardware. Data retention. Security. Audits. Checklist.

PART THREE
Design   127

8. System Specification I   129
Definition and function. Writer. Audience. Good work habits. Parts of the system specification: Title page and table of contents. Problem and solution statement. Charts and diagrams. Checklist.

9. System Specification II   161
Data dictionaries, files, records, and fields. Processing controls. Program narratives. Operating characteristics. Restrictions and trade-offs. Costs and schedules. System test plan. Checklist.

PART FOUR
Implementation   207

10. User's Manual   209
Definition and function. Writer. Audience. Work habits. Outline. Writing suggestions. Checklist.

PART FIVE
Informal Writings   235

11. Memoranda, Status Reports, Minutes, Summaries   237
Memoranda. Status reports. Minutes. Summaries. Checklist.

PART SIX
Conclusion   263

Index   **265**

Preface

This book is about the writing of different documents that accompany the development and implementation of a computer system. Anyone can learn to write good documentation from this book. It is written for computer scientists who design and implement systems, for technical writers who document systems, for supervisors who are responsible for delivering systems, and for clients who must know whether the system delivered is suitable and well documented.

The book is designed for classroom use in colleges, universities or vocational schools and for in-house use in employee development programs in business, industry or government. It is also useful as a self-study program and as a reference book.

Here are the distinguishing features of the book.

1. The book joins the disciplines of Computing Science and English by applying good writing standards to documenting a computer system. One does not need to be a specialist in the other field to learn from this book. The interdisciplinary approach makes this text useful both to English Departments for composition courses focusing on interfacing with computer systems and to Computing Science Departments for courses in documentation or as a companion text in systems courses.
2. Examples illustrate each document and parts of each document. The examples deliberately show both good and bad writing because one must be able to judge writing from the reader's point-of-view to become a good writer. One must also learn to judge writing in order to know ways to correct and improve ineffective writing.
3. All examples have an author's comment. Therefore, the reader is not left to wonder if his or her evaluation of an example is sound but can make a comparison.
4. The format and organization of the book combine to make the text easy to read, understand, and use. The design cleanly separates the examples, the author's comments, and the text.

The format of the text allows one to see how particular information relates to or is separate from other information as discussed in the text regarding stages of system development, the documents within those stages, each document and individual parts of each document.

5. A checklist closes each chapter. It serves both as a summary and a reference. An index permits easy access to the text and provides cross-reference information.

I wish to acknowledge those who helped make this book possible:

- My Composition 316 students who commented on and contributed to the many examples in the text
- Manfred W. Schauss who read the initial chapters and encouraged me to continue writing
- William F. Herrin to whom I continually turned for answers on technical questions
- Dean John R. Tooley and Department Chairman William M. Mitchell who supported my developing a course in documentation which resulted in my writing this book
- Terry Hill, Director of Information Systems, Welborn Baptist Hospital, who kindly helped with information about system documentation in a real-world setting
- Brete Harrison, my editor, who made this book possible and who cared about the quality of the work
- Candace Demeduc, Editorial Assistant to Mr. Harrison, for her help, support, and good cheer
- Editors who read and made constructive comments, particularly CJ Puotinen for her careful reading
- Cobb/Dunlop Publisher Services for copyediting and Jennie Nichols/ Levavi & Levavi for giving the manuscript its form and design.

To each of these, I thank you.

Ann Stuart

WRITING AND ANALYZING EFFECTIVE COMPUTER SYSTEM DOCUMENTATION

PART ONE

INTRODUCTION

1
You, Writing, and System Documentation

It is easy to find people who agree that good documentation is essential to a computer system. It is also easy to find those who agree that there is a need for better system documentation within the computer industry. It is difficult, however, to find people who agree on how the need can be met. Some say that documentation takes time that is too costly to spend writing. Others comment that the different kinds of writing, the different writers involved, and the different people who read and use the documentation make writing effective documentation such a complex task that no solution seems practical.

No single solution can be a cure-all for the many problems of effectively documenting a computer system, but good writing is a useful antidote. Well-written documents are carefully thought out, accurately and precisely presented, and organized so that they read easily. Such characteristics improve the quality of documentation.

Good writing is also a practical solution because the ability to write effective computer system documentation can be learned and improved. It does not require a talent like that necessary to be a great novelist or poet. Instead, if you understand what you are to write and how to write it, and if you practice writing and evaluating your work, you can be a good writer and a constructive critic. Whether you are the programmer/analyst, the project manager, the manager of systems programming, the manager of a software house that develops and sells documentation, the user, or the client who is requesting or purchasing the documentation, you need to know how to write and evaluate system documentation. You then will know if what you are producing or considering is of good quality.

Of course, you already know how to write and have already studied writing in other situations. From your experience, you know that writing is a task you perform alone. Naturally, you can discuss your ideas with others, or you can ask others how they write, or you can attend a writing class. But when you sit down to write, you must do it yourself. Recognizing this fact, this book teaches techniques of self-instruction. You learn to make decisions that cause you to be a better writer, and you learn to analyze documentation so that you become a good critic.

The basis of this learning is the application of standard tools of English composition to computer system documentation. The good of this approach is that it is timeless. System development may change, the documents themselves may change, the work you do and your job may change, but English composition standards do not.

Stages and Documents of Computer System Development

Computer system development traditionally falls into three stages: analysis, design, and implementation. At the conclusion of each major step in the system development cycle, a formal document is written. These documents form the basis of our study:

Stage of System Development	**Document Generated**
I. Analysis	1. Proposal
	2. Functional specification
II. Design	1. System specification
	2. Program specification
III. Implementation	1. Manuals: user and operational
	2. Updating procedures

We will study a document by first asking how it relates to the whole system. Then we will ask how it relates to the segment in which it belongs: analysis, design, or implementation. Finally we will consider how its parts relate to each other to form the document itself.

This approach makes you look first at the forest in order to see the place of each tree, to see first the whole before looking at the parts.

Parts are not a true picture. A reminder of this truth is the lesson of the Indian riddle, "The Four Blind Men." Four blind men approached, for the first time, an elephant. One touched the elephant's leg and said, "It's a log." Another grabbed the tail and cried, "It's a rope." A third stroked the elephant's ear and exclaimed, "It's a fan." A fourth reached out and felt the body and shouted, "It's something without a beginning or end."

If the system design team approaches system documentation like the blind men in this tale, the same misunderstanding can occur. One can grab the "ear" and cry, "I have the problem." That person will start designing solutions. Another may grasp the "tail" and shout, "I have the solution." That one will begin coding programs. Another may be like the man who came up against the "body"; that one will analyze and design without a beginning or end. Each is

1 YOU, WRITING, AND SYSTEM DOCUMENTATION

beginning without understanding the whole. Not one is a careful problem solver.

The goal is to have each document in each stage of analysis, design, and implementation interrelate for easy comprehension. Furthermore, the parts of each individual report must work together to state correctly the function of that single report. How to do this successfully is the subject of this book.

2
A Handbook for the Writer and Critic

Rules to Remember

This chapter is a handbook both for working through the material of this book and for using afterwards as a reference. The rules and patterns identified have their source in the art of rhetoric and exposition which is as old as the Greeks and is familiar to you from other experiences with writing. In high school, technical school, or college, you took basic writing courses that taught the essay and focused on organization, grammar, and content. These were courses in exposition, or writing that informs. You learned rules and rhetorical patterns for organizing and stating your ideas quickly and clearly. In this course of study, you will apply the same rules and patterns to analyzing, writing, and evaluating computer information.

You will learn ways to structure your approach to writing. You will eliminate or quickly answer preliminary questions you once asked anew for every documentation task. You will acquire patterns for presenting material which let you make effective decisions about presentation or style or format.

You will also become a constructive critic. A critic's role is to recognize ineffective documentation and offer ways to correct it. This book establishes criteria for making these evaluations. You may apply your ability to analyze to your own writing or to the writing of others.

✓ 1. Analyze the Document

Each document of a computer system has its own function, and there can even be separate functions for the individual parts of any one document. (A discussion of function is a part of each chapter on individual documents.) Begin document analysis by determining purpose. If you know what the document is supposed to do, you can work out ways for it to do that. For example, a proposal's function is to persuade. Knowing this, you can begin by considering persuasive approaches like the following.

A. One way to begin is to tell the history of the problem the proposal intends to solve. Such an approach often works because you establish your credibility if you present the history accurately. But this approach has some obvious hazards. One is that the reader can become bored and stop reading before you have the opportunity to present your idea.

Example 1

The writing in this example is too particular.

Introduction to a Proposal for Changing a Membership File

Introduction: Channel X TV and the Radio Station continually conduct membership analysis. These stations also conduct fund drives two to three times a year to acquire new members. Presently a master file, maintained and implemented at the local business college, is used to produce mailing lists. The records on this master file contain the names, addresses, pledge date, and code (codes based on ranges set by the station) for each member. In conjunction with this master file, Ms. S., subscription manager for the station, manually maintains a ledger of all members who pay by monthly installments. The ledgers contain personal data, ID number, initial pledge amount, a running paid-to-date column, and a still-owed column. She also maintains a card file of the total membership, active and inactive. The card file contains the history of each member including personal data, ID number (generated upon initial payment data), initial pledge amount and amount paid to date. The membership department at Channel X wishes to move its master file from the business college to the university because the university has more storage space for member information and reports. Ms. S. would then be able to monitor payments and to view upon request how well members are responding to their pledge amounts and dates. The following points are presented for consideration of this proposed change. . . .

COMMENT
This introduction is flawed by too much detail about "files" and "ledgers," which the reader does not need or want to know at this time.

PART ONE INTRODUCTION

An effective introduction to a proposal shows a problem or need. It persuades the reader to accept the idea being offered. In this example, the long explanation of the present system supposedly contains the problem, but it is ineffectively stated. The reader's interest should be piqued early about why a change should occur and what specific benefits will result.

"More storage space," "to monitor," and "to view" should be defined and explained.

B. Another effective way to use the historical approach is to make the background relevant to the problem and to write briskly and pointedly.

Example 2

This example also presents background material, but it does so more effectively.

Introduction to a Model Shop Management Information System

(1) Currently, no efficient method exists at Company X to consolidate information about each Model Shop Request (MSR). Therefore, separate departments retain complete records of information for each project being worked on and for those under consideration. The effect is that a MSR with multiple accounts appears to the model shop as "multiple requests." Redundancies result in the operational areas of data capture, processing, storage, and reporting.

(2) Furthermore, all information obtained by the model shop is handled on a daily basis by the managers and is a time-consuming job with the following problems:

1. All hours, percentages, etc., are presently computed and recorded by hand for each MSR number.
2. Some data are incorrectly calculated or recorded because of human error.
3. "Daily transactions" take upwards of 1½ hours to complete, leaving less time for other areas of work.
4. Managers often receive handwritten reports 2 or 3 weeks after they are initiated. This is sometimes too late to apply any corrective measures to a problem.

The proposed system will resolve the above identified problem areas by incorporating the following: . . .

COMMENT

Good Points: The explanation of the current way of doing things is coupled with comments about problems or misinterpretations. The first sentence is strong, and the first paragraph identifies a problem. The reader's interest is caught by the directness of the statements.

In addition, the format is effective. Instead of one long paragraph, as in the previous example, the information is broken up into short paragraphs. Listing the "problems" in paragraph 2 makes them easy to see and read. Writing the "problems" in parallel structure (each item begins with a subject/verb structure) is good form.

C. A third persuasive approach is to shock or startle the reader into attention. Writing about money or productivity often does this.

Example 3

This example is direct and effective.

Introduction to a Proposal to Replace a Punched Card System with a CRT Terminal System

Currently, the university is using a card system as input to the computer. This system, including keypunches, card readers, and punched cards, is outdated and unnecessarily expensive. The mechanical equipment is prone to breakdowns, and punched cards are a major expense since they are not reusable. The card system also is not fast enough to satisfy our computing needs. In other words, our computer input system is obsolete.

COMMENT

The confidence and bluntness of the statement is good. The reader will certainly want proof of these claims, but will continue reading because the writer speaks with authority and wastes no time.

Suggestion: To be really blunt and gain attention, place the last sentence first: "Our computer input system is obsolete."

When you act as a critic, also begin document analysis by determining purpose. First, ask what the document is to do. Then decide whether the writer has the same purpose in mind. If not, is the writer's perception equally legitimate, or must you discuss the question of function before proceeding with the project?

For example, if the document is a manual, the purpose is to instruct a particular group of users. You must decide how well it does this. A manual that cannot be used is worthless. If you are the manager of the documentation project, or the client who is buying the manual, or the software house that is marketing the manual, "worthless" is expensive. By disciplining yourself to evaluate in an orderly manner and by developing a set of criteria, you will increase your own effectiveness and better serve those whose work you evaluate.

✔ 2. Analyze the Audience

Whether you are writer or critic, you must know your audience. The people who read your documents are the same people with whom you do business. Certainly you adjust your manner, tone, vocabulary, and information to suit those you speak with. You must do the same when you write or evaluate writing.

Ask yourself who is to read the work. Is the reader friendly or hostile? Is it one reader or several? Do the readers have a common level of understanding? If not, decide how you are going to write so all who need the information can understand it. Interview or observe or do research, but learn about the reader.

A. The subject of audience is discussed in each chapter, but to consider a common problem in audience analysis, think of a group of readers who know different things. For readers who do not have technical knowledge, you may need to provide a glossary. Or you may decide to begin your report with a general statement directed to a general audience and follow it with technical discussions directed to specific people with special interests and knowledge. In another instance, you may define your audience so that anyone who does not fit the profile will know this document is not directed to his or her level of experience.

Example 4

This work effectively identifies those qualified to use a manual for Solving Linear Programming Problems Using the Graphical Method:

```
Project Users:

1. Students who have been introduced to the graphical method of
   solving LP problems through classroom lecture
2. Students who have at least a general knowledge of college-
   level algebra
3. Students who have been instructed on the use of the Apple II
   Plus computer and are familiar with the procedures for run-
   ning programs on diskette
```

COMMENT
The qualifications for "Project Users" are clear and definite. A student with none of these qualifications obviously cannot use the manual. This is a simple yet effective way to identify your audience.

    B. Audience analysis also involves choosing tone and vocabulary. Just as you vary your speech when you talk formally or informally, you must adjust your language to different clients or users or managers.

Example 5

This statement is from an introduction to a proposal that suggests developing a guide for selecting a small computer system. A poor word choice hurts the writing.

> The small business person buys a small computer system only to find that the system is completely wrong for the type of work performed.

COMMENT
Both the choice and placement of "small" are poor. Naturally, in the first reference, "small" does not mean a "little" person, but it can be read that way; it also does not mean "small-minded," but it can suggest that. In the second reference, "small" is relative. What is a small business to one person will not be to another. This language could offend and turn away the reader.

Example 6

The following statement belongs to a proposal to use a Microcomputer System to Increase Secretarial Productivity.

> We must either increase the secretarial manpower available or increase the productivity of the secretaries.

COMMENT
Imagine how this proposal will be received by "unproductive" secretaries who may have access to this report. Also imagine how women secretaries will respond to "secretarial manpower." The tone needs to be corrected because the writer did not mean to insult the secretaries. The example illustrates our need to be sensitive to how our words appear to others.

PART ONE INTRODUCTION

Example 7

This statement comes from the first draft of a proposal to install an Optical Scanning System for three area liquor stores. A rewrite follows that alters the tone.

> Control over the business seems to be the primary concern and is exercised to the extent that your present system allows. Some of your present procedures seem to have endured the test of time dating back to 1946 when X Liquor was a one-store operation on X and Y Road.

COMMENT
A friendly tone is often effective, but this "good old boy" tone about the "one-store operation" is not good, professional writing. Besides, some people do not appreciate being reminded of their business beginnings. The writer takes an unnecessary risk in being so familiar. The statement that the business methods have "endured the test of time" also implies that they have not been updated. This suggestion may offend.

The statement was rewritten to read:

> Control over the business seems to be the primary concern to management and is exercised to the extent that your present system allows. While the system in use is obviously working, we have found some opportunities for improvement.

COMMENT
The tone is less personal and more professional. The statement is improved. The writer has found a way to compliment ("the system . . . is obviously working") yet to offer improvements.

✔ 3. Organize and Outline

Know before you begin to write how you are going to proceed. How many parts will make up the report? How are the parts labeled? In what order are you going to present them? Your initial analysis of the document and the audience help answer such questions. For instance, if the document is a manual and its function is to instruct users with no experience, you must be very complete and very clear. You may need to show alternative routes if something goes wrong in the process, or loops of action, or give other information to aid the user. The experience level of the audience and complexity of the task being taught influence the order of presentation.

One means of ordering your information is to make an outline of your plan. It lets you see where you are going, where the problems are, and what changes you should make. The outline also allows you to see the report as a whole; you can thereby better interrelate the parts.

It is useful to show the outline to someone else, because in its skeletal stage the parts of the document are clearly visible. A reader can spot illogical connections or omissions. At this stage, corrections are less time-consuming and costly than they are later.

Outlining helps you schedule. Often, as you write the parts of the document, your scope changes. If it becomes smaller, you have no problem, but if it grows larger, the outline prompts you to begin, set milestones, and set aside time. Developing this habit makes you better prepared. Fewer last-minute crises will occur.

Obviously it is neither possible nor practical to prepare formal outlines for every writing task. But the habit of outlining should be developed. Jot down major parts even if you do not prepare a formal outline.

The outline also can serve double duty. Once you write it, it can be used later as the table of contents.

Example 8

This table of contents for a Pharmacy Information System is simple, yet it is complete and specifically titled so a reader can use it effectively. It also is a useful outline for the writer.

```
                    Table of Contents
Introduction
Statement of Problem
Design Approach
Hardware Selection
Results
Conclusion and Recommendations
Appendix A: File System
Appendix B: Data Flow Diagrams
Appendix C: Structure Charts
Appendix D: Data Dictionary
Appendix E: User's Manual
```

To a manager, client, or anyone else acting as critic, an outline is essential to efficiency and cost effectiveness. It lets you determine whether the document will satisfy the need before you waste the writer's time on something that is wrongly directed.

PART ONE INTRODUCTION

✔ 4. Format Effectively

Plot the information on the page. Arrange words so the most important parts of the report are clearly seen. Use capitalization, underlining, double striking, numbering, color, or placement to separate material. When the reader first picks up the report and glances through it, he or she should be able to sense its organization and to find the critical information.

Format with psychological as well as intellectual impact in mind. No one looks forward to reading a page crammed with words. Allow space. Create variety. Do not make your text look dull.

As a critic, you often evaluate documents that must be attractively formatted. Even when an appealing arrangement is not essential, it indicates your attitude about you, those who work for you, and your business. It shows that you care about detail and about appearance.

Example 9

The two examples that follow illustrate two differently formatted pages, but each is a good example of attractive spacing. The information in both is easy to read and reference.

Example 9A

```
INTRODUCTION
    The Pharmacy Information System is designed to fulfill the
needs of X Drug Store, a small pharmacy operation in Perry,
Florida. Mr. X., the owner, has been unable to find a commer-
cial, cost-effective package to meet his procedural require-
ments.
    The system requirements include management of a large (by
typical small-business computer standards) and unique data
base; use of the data base to perform the operations associated
with prescription processing (including label preparation,
price calculation according to several different schedules,
and preparation of insurance forms); and ease of use by an inex-
perienced user.
```

COMMENT
While the format is effective, this sentence with two semicolons and two sets of parentheses is not easy to read. Make the writing as clear as the format.

```
In its present state, the file system has the capabilities of
create, add, alter, delete, and update. The system also proces-
ses prescriptions and prepares three types of insurance forms.
```

STATEMENT OF THE PROBLEM

X's is a small pharmacy operation which processes approximately 14,000 prescriptions per year. Data must be available for approximately 16,000 pharmaceutical products, 14,000 prescriptions, 8,000 patients, and 150 physicians. Processing is most efficient if this information is readily available.

As an additional customer service, three types of insurance forms <u>are provided</u>. For each customer, a medication history <u>is maintained</u>, a feature which many commercial systems do not provide.

Presently, all processing described above <u>is done</u> manually. All <u>could be handled</u> efficiently and accurately with a <u>small</u> business computer. Employees would then be free for other work.

COMMENT

It is not necessary to write every sentence in active voice, but it does create a vigorous and direct style because the subject does the action of the verb. As the critic of this work, I suggest rewriting to active voice the sentences with underlined verbs. Examples:

> Passive voice: As an additional customer service, three types of insurance forms <u>are provided</u>. [The subject ("types") is acted upon. It receives the action.]
> Active voice: X Drug Store provides three types of insurance forms as an additional customer service. [The subject ("store") performs the action ("provides").]
> Passive voice: For each customer, a medication history <u>is maintained</u>, a feature which many commercial systems do not provide. [The subject ("history") is acted upon. It receives the action.]
> Active voice: The store maintains a medication history for each customer. [The subject ("store") performs the action ("maintains").]

DESIGN APPROACH

The Pharmacy System was designed around the data base, which consists of four main files: the patient-profile file, the drug file, the doctor file, and prescription file. The patient-profile file is indexed and has a subsidiary history file for medication history. The file management system is described in Appendix A.

Example 9B

```
              MERIT AWARDS SYSTEM
             APPLICATION INFORMATION
              FUNCTION SPECIFICATIONS


    SYSTEM:    MERIT AWARDS SYSTEM
    PROGRAM:   PNSUPD53
    FUNCTION:  AWARD MONTHLY POINTS
    FEATURES:  1. Validates the user's password.
               2. Determines from the user's response
                  whether to give the monthly points to
                  eligible safety award employees who
                  have not had an accident.

                  Exception:
                     Do not award monthly points to sala-
                     ried office employees (work group
                     #999999) and supervisors who are not
                     members of a work group (work group
                     #0).

    FORMSFILE: PNFSUP53/PNFFUP53
    DATA SETS: AWARDS, DETAIL, DETAIL, (1/)
```

COMMENT
Careful arrangement makes this information easy to read and use, two benefits that make effective formatting worthwhile.

5. Be Responsible for What You Write

No one will be impressed or convinced by generalizations, faulty logic or sloppy work. Do not promise what you cannot deliver. Do not state facts you have not checked.

Example 10

In this example, the writer fails to say whether any of the proposed suggestions are tied down. He or she provides no verification regarding space or personnel or money pledged to this project. The "requirements" seem like a dream list.

Operational Requirements:

The School of Business Administration (S.B.A.) would like to see the Satellite Center for Data Processing be developed as follows:

1. A room (at least 1200 square feet within close proximity to the S.B.A. office) designated to contain the Satellite Center

COMMENT
Is such a room available? Will someone or some office be displaced? Will the person or persons agree to move? If not, can the writer obtain the authority to have the office made available?

2. This room remodeled to provide the proper work environment

COMMENT
What does "remodeling" mean? Painting? Electrical work? Other work? Is the money budgeted?

3. A line-printer of reasonable speed purchased and installed

COMMENT
What is "reasonable?" How is reasonable determined? By whom? Is the money available to purchase this item? If not, how is the money to be raised?

4. Three portable, dial-up terminals for use in classroom demonstration installed

COMMENT
Where do they go and has that space been approved?

5. Responsibility for operation and control of Satellite Center carried out by personnel from academic computing

COMMENT
How many people? Is this agreed to or must it be negotiated?

6. Twenty CRT terminals installed

COMMENT
Installed where? Is everything ready for installation? If not, what has to be done? Who installs? Who pays?

SUMMARY COMMENT
The writer needs either to state that permissions, money, personnel, and space have been obtained and the project is feasible, or to check and secure such items before writing. For a project to be reliable and worth discussing, it must be real. You must be specific about what has been done and what is still to be done. Do not write about ideas you cannot make happen.

6. Look at Your Words

Have you selected language that states precisely and accurately what you mean to say? Using the same word over and over can suggest a paucity of thought. Look at your verbs, nouns, and descriptive words. Consult the dictionary. Is there a more explicit, more vivid way to write your information? If so, rewrite and use a better word or image.

Rivers of murky, polluted, stagnant reports flood our desks every day. Clean up your reports. Become a language environmentalist!

Example 11

A rewrite follows this example of murky, redundant prose:

> In the modern business world there is a great need for managers in various specialized business fields who are also capable of working with computers. The amount of people who are qualified in both business areas is very small. As a result many of these jobs are filled with people who are qualified in the specialized fields, but who are not qualified in the computer fields. Many business managers are faced with decisions dealing with all types of computer problems.

Rewrite to say simply:

> Business managers need to understand both business practices and the use of computers.

COMMENT
Schedule time to prune and shape your writing. Make it speak well for you.

7. Proofread: If Necessary, Rewrite or Retype ✓

Problems often look different after a good night's sleep. So can your report. If it seems wordy or vague or disorganized when you come back to it, fix it. Pay attention to grammar, punctuation, and spelling. If you are not sure about a word, look it up, Do not send out a document that is poorly written or poorly typed. An error-filled report calls into question all else that you have written.

Example 12

Think how you might judge the writer of this unchecked report.

OUTPUT REPORTS FORMATS: A printer spacing chart is used in this report to illustrate the reports generated by the edit procedures and the update prodeudres. Each line of the actual report

is recorded on the spacing chart as it appears on that report. The reports can be classisfied into three catogories, edit listing, update listings, and update listings fesulting from

the tatal records update. One the printer spacing chart X's represent character data, 9's represent numerical data, and Zs represent zera supressed numerical data.

Text marked for errors

OUTPUT REPORT$ FORMAT$: A ⓟrinter Ⓢpacing Ⓒhart is used in this *What is "illustrated"--*
report (to illustrate) the reports generated by the edit proce-   *the "reports" or the "edit" and "update procedures"?*
dures and the update prodⒺuⒹdres. Each line of the actual report
is recorded on the Ⓢpacing Ⓒhart as it appears on that report.) *Inconsistent*
The reports can be classiⓈfied into three catⒺgoriesⓄⒿedit   *spacing*
listingⓈ, update listings, and update listings(Ⓓesulting from)
the tⒽtal records update). OnⒺ the ⓟrinter Ⓢpacing ⒸhartⓄX's
represent character data, 9's represent numerical data, and ZⓈⒺ
represent zerⒶsupⓟressed numerical data.

COMMENT
Such a report was distributed. No writer should be so careless.

CHECKLIST: CHAPTER 2
Rules to Remember

1.	ANALYZE DOCUMENT	Know its purpose. Fit approach to purpose.
2.	ANALYZE AUDIENCE	Know who is to read the document. Adjust tone and vocabulary to suit audience. Write to the audience's level of knowledge. Provide ways to satisfy readers who know different things.
3.	ORGANIZE AND OUTLINE	Have an overview before you begin. Make the parts fit the whole. Use an outline.
4.	FORMAT EFFECTIVELY	Plot information so it is easy to read and use. Arrange information attractively.
5.	BE RESPONSIBLE FOR WHAT YOU SAY	Check your information. Say only what you can produce. Do not generalize.
6.	LOOK AT YOUR WORDS	Be a language environmentalist—clean up your reports.
7.	PROOFREAD, REWRITE, RETYPE	Allow time to revise. Submit error-free reports.

3
Structures for Writing

Structure Your Writing

Methods of "structuring" your documentation are built into the patterns of rhetoric. These patterns are the same ones useful to you in writing other informative communications; the only difference is that now you are going to apply them to your computer documentation:

1. Definition
2. Comparison and Contrast
3. Classification and Division
4. Description
5. Narration
6. Process Analysis
7. Procedure
8. Cause and Effect
9. Persuasion

Separate definitions explain each pattern. Use any one or any combination to write your documentation.

1. Definition ✔

A definition explains something precisely. Clear definitions allow diverse groups (personnel managers, programmers, hardware specialists, users, finance managers, etc.) to speak the same language as they meet to develop and implement effective computer systems.

HOW TO WRITE A DEFINITION

Know Your Purpose: Are you defining something in a new way? Defining a new idea for the first time? Defining an idea with many meanings in a particular way?

Know Your Audience: What do your readers already understand? How much do you want them to know?

Structure Your Definitions: Traditional patterns for defining include the following:

Analogy: Define one thing by naming another that means the same thing. Define a new or difficult idea by a familiar or easy one:
"A computer storage unit is like a file cabinet. It is capable of storing information in an orderly manner."

Etymology: State the root of the word to help the reader understand the term:
"A proposal can be identified by its name: The root 'poser' means to place or put, and the prefix 'pro' means forth. Therefore, a proposal is a bid for work that you put forth."

Class and Difference: Assign the term/item to a class; explain how the term/item differs from others in the same class. The difference must apply only to the term/item being defined, not to any others in the class:

Term	Class	Individual Difference
microcomputer	computers	(a unique point)

Analysis: Define in general; then divide into parts:
"A development cycle is. . . ."
"A cycle consists of a series of actions known as analysis, design, and implementation."

Characteristics: Define by giving specific features:
"The distinguishing characteristics of structured English are. . . ."

Elimination: Define by telling what something is not:
"A computer system is not a. . . ."

Extended Definition: Use any or all of the previous methods to construct a definition.

Things to Avoid: Do not write in circles; do not use the same words for both the idea you are defining and its definition. Do not be too general; precise information is critical to good computer writing and analysis.

Example 13

This writer defines the problem by using "analysis," first stating the problem generally, then dividing it into two parts.

PROBLEM DEFINITION

Each time a weaver envisions a pattern for a piece of cloth, the actual weaving must be delayed until the weaver completes preliminary tasks. Problems exist within these "preludes to weaving" in manual pattern drafting (draw-down) and in yarn quantity calculations for the finished piece.

Problems with the manual drafting or the draw-down:

1. Causes time-consuming design methods
2. Lacks ease of modification to the draw-down

Problems with the calculations of yarn quantities:

1. Causes mathematical computations to be tedious
2. Lacks ease of adaptation to changes in variables

COMMENT

The definition is precise and useful. The reader understands the problems and can go forward to read about proposed solutions. Careful structuring helps state the definition simply and clearly.

Example 14

In this excerpt, the writer effectively uses "characteristics" to define the personnel system:

Definition of Terms

ACCUMULATED POINTS	Total accumulated award points
ALPHA SEARCH KEY	Alphabetical search key
BIRTH DATE	Employee's date of birth (MM/DD/YY)
BONUS POINTS	Bonus award points earned this month
BRANCH	Branch location of employee

```
            CITY/STATE              City and state where employee
                                    resides
            DENTAL INSURANCE        Dental insurance coverage
                                    F=Family
                                    S=Single
                                    N=None
```

COMMENT
Each item is specifically identified so no overlap or ambiguity is possible. The method of defining is effective and efficient.

2. Comparison and Contrast

The process of comparing one thing to another is so common to your experience that it seems almost unnecessary to talk formally about doing it; yet because it is so common, you must compare effectively.

To compare is to show how two of anything are alike; to contrast is to show how they differ. You do not always have to show both. The reason for making the comparison dictates what to include.

Comparison and contrast are used for many different purposes. For example, you can instruct by showing how two things are similar and dissimilar; you can provide information so that others can choose, recommend, or evaluate by comparing one item with another; you can examine two of anything to see how they are alike or different.

HOW TO WRITE USING COMPARISON AND CONTRAST

Make a Point: You must have a reason for making the comparison. State it.

Be Complete and Fair: Include all relevant points of comparison even though some may not support your preference.

Structure Your Material: Two basic patterns of organization are available. Choose one and stay with that structure for the complete comparison.

1. Block Method: Present all information about the first subject, then the second subject. Cover the same information for both subjects and present the material in the same order:

 FORTRAN
  General User
  Ease of Learning
  Readability
  Capabilities

COBOL
    General User
    Ease of Learning
    Readability
    Capabilities

COMMENT
This pattern is most effective when you want the reader to consider the two subjects separately. The reader sorts out the likenesses and differences in order to choose, recommend, use, purchase, etc. This pattern's disadvantage appears when a lot of information is presented. It is difficult to remember all the points in order to compare the two subjects thoroughly. The reader has to flip back and forth, which is awkward and irritating.

2. Point-by-Point: Identify a point of comparison. Then apply each point to subject 1 and subject 2:

GENERAL USER
    Fortran
    Cobol

EASE OF LEARNING
    Fortran
    Cobol

READABILITY
    Fortran
    Cobol

CAPABILITIES
    Fortran
    Cobol

COMMENT
This pattern is most effective when you want the reader to consider two things at the same time. The points of comparison are easy to see.
    To select which pattern to use, ask yourself: Do I want to emphasize the two subjects or the points of comparison?

PART ONE INTRODUCTION

✔ 3. Classification and Division

When you examine three or more items in order to explain their connections, you are classifying and dividing.

   Classification examines one thing as a part of a class or group; it looks up; it moves from specific to general; it relates something to the big picture.

   Division examines the different parts of one thing; it looks down; it moves from general to specific; it narrows the vision in order to look at something carefully.

HOW TO WRITE A CLASSIFICATION AND/OR DIVISION

Make a Point: Have a reason for classifying or dividing. State it. Follow it.

Establish a Unifying Principle: Use only one basis for classification and division at a time. Stay with it.

Concentrate: Because the organizational task is more complicated, you must be careful. Remember the basis of your classification and/or division and always write to that point.

Example 15

The following two examples illustrate how to organize classification and division.

Example 15A

	Programming Languages			→ *Class*
Machine	*Assembly*	*High-level*		→ *Item*
immense amount of detail required	symbolic abbreviations reduce detail	a few English-like terms are expanded by a compiler into a large number of detailed instructions		→ *Characteristics* that distinguish each item from others in the class

• *Unifying Principle:* Detail

Example 15B

```
              Printers                  →  Class
         ┌───────┼───────┐
      Serial   Line    Page             →  Item

      prints   prints  prints           →  Characteristics
      single   entire  entire              that distinguish
      character line at page                each item from
      at a time a time  at a time           others in the
                                            class

                                        • Unifying
                                          Principle: Amount
                                          of information
                                          printed each
                                          cycle
```

Example 16

The following example effectively divides the Management Information System (MIS) by using jobs as the unifying principle. The "charts" are not included in the example.

It is always good practice to divide a large job into smaller pieces that can be easily understood. To that end, the overall MIS job divides into the following parts:

1. *Customers:*
   One important objective of the MIS will be to obtain and document customer participation as explained in the attached chart labeled "A." "Customers" refers to the identification of the individual or department requesting the model shop work.
2. *Project/Work Request:*
   The documentation of all relevant transactions associated with a given project and work request will be an integral part of the MIS as indicated on chart "B."
3. *Model Shop:*
   Internal documentation of model shop activities is within the scope of the MIS. An example might be model shop hours estimated vs. hours worked on a specific project. See chart "C."

4. *Parts/Services:*
   Documentation of the output or results of the model shop operation is important. See chart "D."
5. *Resources:*
   Of potential interest to the MIS are external resources required to operate the model shop—for example, molds from X Lumber or raw materials. See chart "E."
6. *Observer:*
   The overall interaction of the customer, project work request, model shop, and parts and services system is of interest to top management, accounting, and corporate engineering. See chart "F."

COMMENT

The reason for the division is to identify the areas of documentation that the MIS will monitor. A reader sees at a glance the different areas of documentation, is given examples of the information documented, and has a chart to refer to for further information. The writer is consistent and uses division properly to explain how different kinds of documentation collected relate to the Management Information System.

Example 17

If the writer classifies several items with several divisions, the reader can have difficulty sorting and using the information. The following example illustrates such a situation and presents an effective solution.

In the example, the writer divides data processing languages according to their characteristics in order to help consultants choose the language that best suits their customers' needs.

FIRST DRAFT

A first draft follows. The writer organizes well, divides the languages and their characteristics consistently, and formats with lots of white space. But the report is a disaster to use. Readers who want to consider "numeric operators" (II.A) must riffle through the many pages to find that information on each language and then somehow hold those pages in order to flip back and forth to evaluate. The reader is certainly going to be aggravated and most likely will avoid using the report.

ADA LANGUAGE FEATURES:
  I. DATA TYPES
     A. Primitives
        1. Integer
        2. Real
        3. Boolean
        4. Character
        5. Void
     B. Non-primitives
        1. Arrays   Single and Multiple Dimension
        2. Pointers
        3. Tables
        4. Records
        5. Queues
     C. User-defined
     D. Built-in
        1. Null
 II. OPERATORS
     A. Numeric Operators
        1. + Addition
        2. − Subtraction
        3. / Division
        4. * Multiplication
        5. **Exponentiation
     B. Relational Operators
        1. <
        2. >
        3. =
     C. Boolean Operators
        1. And
        2. Or
        3. Not
        4. Xor   Exclusive Or
III. CHARACTER MANIPULATION FUNCTIONS
     Not Available
 IV. CONTROL STRUCTURES
        1. If Then Else
        2. For In Loop
        3. While Loop
        4. Loop
        5. Do End
        6. Goto
        7. Case of

PART ONE   INTRODUCTION

    V. FILE STRUCTURES
       Not Available
   VI. STRUCTURING TECHNIQUES
      1. Subprograms
      2. Functions
      3. Procedures
  VII. SELF-DOCUMENTATION
      1. English-like Words
      2. Underlining Keywords
      3. User-defined Data Names
      4. Indentation-for Clarity
      5. Comments—beginning with—and runs to the end of the line
 VIII. LOGIC ANALYSIS SUPPORT
      Not Available

COBOL LANGUAGE FEATURES:
    I. DATA TYPES
      A. Primitives
        1. Integer
        2. Character
      B. Non-primitives
        1. Record
        2. Table   Single and Multiple Dimensions
          a. Subscript
          b. Index
   II. OPERATORS
      A. Numeric Operators
        1. Add
        2. Subtract
        3. Multiply
        4. Divide
        5. Compute
          a. + Addition
          b. − Subtraction
          c. * Multiplication
          d. / Division
          e. **Exponentiation
      B. Relational Operators
        1. Greater
        2. Equal
        3. Less
        4. >

               5. =
               6. <
           C. Boolean Operators
               1. And
               2. Or
               3. Not
           D. Sign Operators
               1. Positive
               2. Zero
               3. Negative
           E. Class Operators
               1. Numeric
               2. Alphabetic
   III. CHARACTER MANIPULATION FUNCTIONS
               1. Examine
               2. Inspect
               3. String
               4. Unstring
    IV. CONTROL STRUCTURES
               1. If Then Else
               2. Go to
               3. Perform
                   a. Varying From
                   b. By Until
     V. FILE STRUCTURES
               1. Indexed Random
               2. Indexed Sequential
               3. Sequential
               4. Direct
    VI. STRUCTURING TECHNIQUES
               1. Subroutines
                   a. Internal
                   b. External
   VII. SELF-DOCUMENTATION
               1. English-like words
               2. Divisions
                   a. Identification
                   b. Environment
                   c. Data
                   d. Procedure
               3. Paragraphs—Unique Names and Numbers
               4. Labels
                   a. Group
                   b. Elementary

     5. Comments—* In Column 7, Runs to the End of the Line
     6. Indentation—For Clarity
  VIII. LOGIC ANALYSIS SUPPORT
    1. Display
    2. Ready Trace
    3. Exhibit Named
    4. Exhibit Changed
    5. Exhibit Named Changed

PASCAL LANGUAGE FEATURES:
 I. DATA TYPES
  A. Primitives
   1. Integer
   2. Real
   3. Boolean
   4. Character
   5. Void
  B. Non-primitives
   1. Pointer Memory Allocation
   2. Arrays   Single and Multiple Dimension
   3. Structures Record Data Type
  C. User-defined
 II. OPERATORS
  A. Numeric Operators
   1. + Addition
   2. − Subtraction
   3. * Multiplication
   4. DIV Integer Division
   5. / Real Division
  B. Relational Operators
   1. <
   2. >
   3. =
  C. Boolean Operators
   1. And
   2. Or
   3. Not
  D. Set Operators
   1. * Set Intersection
   2. + Set Union
   3. − Set Difference
 III. CHARACTER MANIPULATION FUNCTIONS
  Not Available

        IV. CONTROL STRUCTURES
            1. Do While
            2. Repeat Until
            3. Do I
            4. Subroutines
            5. Functions
            6. If Then Else
            7. Case of
            8. Go to
        V. FILE STRUCTURES
            1. Sequential Files
        VI. STRUCTURING TECHNIQUES
            1. Subroutines   Internal and External
            2. Functions   Internal Only
            3. Recursion
        VII. SELF-DOCUMENTATION
            1. Labels
            2. User-defined Data Names
            3. Comments—begin with a (* and end with a *)
            4. Identation—for Clarity
    VIII. LOGIC ANALYSIS SUPPORT
            Not Available

(This organization continues through the remaining two languages.)

SECOND DRAFT

In this version, the writer finds an effective way to present the same material so that now it is easy to read and use. The example shows the importance of understanding function. The consultants cannot effectively use the first draft. They can the second.

DATA TYPES	ADA	COBOL	PASCAL	PL/1	RPG
Primitives					
Integer	Y	Y	Y	Y	Y
Real	Y		Y	Y	
Boolean	Y		Y	Y	
Character	Y	Y	Y	Y	Y
Void	Y		Y	Y	

DATA TYPES	ADA	COBOL	PASCAL	PL/1	RPG
Non-primitives					
Arrays	Y		Y	Y	Y
Pointers	Y		Y	Y	
Tables	Y	Y			
Records	Y	Y			
Queues	Y				
Structures			Y	Y	
Indicators					Y
User-defined	Y		Y		
Built-in					
Null	Y			Y	

OPERATORS	ADA	COBOL	PASCAL	PL/1	RPG
Numeric					
+	Y	Y	Y	Y	
-	Y	Y	Y	Y	
/	Y	Y	Y	Y	
*	Y	Y	Y	Y	
**	Y	Y		Y	
ADD		Y			Y
SUBTRACT		Y			
MULTIPLY		Y			
DIVIDE		Y			
COMPUTE		Y			
DIV			Y		Y
MULT					Y

OPERATORS	ADA	COBOL	PASCAL	PL/1	RPG
SUB					Y
Z-ADD					Y
Z-SUB					Y
Relational					
>	Y	Y	Y	Y	Y
=	Y	Y	Y	Y	Y
<	Y	Y	Y	Y	Y
GREATER		Y			
EQUAL		Y			
LESS		Y			
Boolean					
AND	Y	Y	Y	Y	Y
OR	Y	Y	Y	Y	Y
NOT	Y	Y	Y	Y	Y
XOR	Y				
Sign					
POSITIVE		Y			
ZERO		Y			
NEGATIVE		Y			
Class					
NUMERIC		Y			
ALPHABETIC		Y			
Set					
*			Y		
+			Y		
-			Y		

OPERATORS	ADA	COBOL	PASCAL	PL/1	RPG
Control					
SETON					Y
SETOFF					Y

CHARACTER MANIPULATION FUNCTIONS	ADA	COBOL	PASCAL	PL/1	RPG
EXAMINE		Y			
INSPECT		Y			
STRING		Y			
UNSTRING		Y			

(This format continues through the remaining information.)

4. Description

Description tells in detail what something is, looks like, or does. All are used in writing effective computer documentation. A client needs to understand what a file is. A user wants to picture an output in order to evaluate it. A manager must know what a program does that is cost-effective and helpful to his or her division.

HOW TO WRITE USING DESCRIPTION

Make a Point: Why are you writing the description? Is someone going to duplicate the subject being described? Will someone recognize and understand what you are describing? Is someone going to approve something based upon your description of what it does? Asking questions forces you to form answers that will cause you to decide what to write.

Begin with a Definition: Use the patterns of definition stated earlier in this chapter to say what something is. Then describe it.

Be Precise and Objective: Technical descriptions demand accuracy. Do not skip any relevant point. Do not assume the reader will fill in. Be fair and impersonal in your description.

Have a Plan: If you describe what something does, determine an order for explaining it, such as least important to most important, or sequential.

3 STRUCTURES FOR WRITING

If you describe what something looks like, organize the description so the reader can visualize it. Start with an overview, or move from front to back, side to side, around the edges, top to bottom, or divide the whole into sections and the sections into sub-parts.

Example 18

This example describes the doctor and drug files of a Pharmacy Information System:

The description begins with a definition, then tells what the files do.
The format gives each function a separate paragraph which makes the information easy to read.
The "layouts" that accompany the description allow the reader to visualize the files.
The verbal and visual descriptions complement each other and communicate the material effectively.

```
Doctor and Drug Files
    The function and structure of these files are alike. Both are
sequential files that are randomly accessed based on a given
day. The key to the Doctor File is the doctor's name. For the Drug
File, the key is drug name and strength. The record count kept in
Record 0 controls the file size. Figure 2 gives the doctor rec-
ord layout. Figure 3 gives the drug record layout.


    List of examples of file access functions:

    Access a record by using a binary search on a given key.
    Change a record by accessing and displaying it field by
        field. The user enters the changes and the record is re-
        written to the same position.
    Delete a record by accessing a record, flagging it for dele-
        tion, and rewriting it.
    Update a file by reading a file, record by record, and re-
        writing nondeleted records compacted into the same file
        space. An updated record count in R0 reflects that the file
        has been compacted.
    Add a record by copying the file, record by record, to back up
        and by inserting the new record in its correct position.
```

Appendix A

FIGURE 2: Doctor File Structure

Doctor → Doctor Record
Name

Record Length: 87 bytes
File Size: Up to 150 records

RECORD LAYOUT

VARIABLE NAME	DESCRIPTION	BYTE LOCATION
DN$	Doctor's Name	1–20
DA$	Street Address	21–40
DC$	City	41–55
DS$	State Code	56–57
DZ$	Zip Code	58–62
DP$	Phone Number	63–74
DD$	DEA Number	75–81
DM$	Medicaid Provider Number	82–86

Byte 87 is carriage return

FIGURE 3: Drug File Structure

Drug → Drug Record
Name

Record Length: 49 bytes
File Size: Up to 150 records

RECORD LAYOUT

VARIABLE NAME	DESCRIPTION	BYTE LOCATION
ND$	Drug Name and Strength	1–25
NN$	NDC Code	26–36
NP$	AWP Price	37–42
NQ$	Standard Quantity	43–48

Byte 49 is carriage return

5. Narration

Even in computer system documentation, "telling" has its place. At different times and in different reports, it is necessary to explain how something is done, how problems occur, or how a process is performed.

Each of these instances requires a narration; you relate a series of closely related happenings, telling the "story" of how or why something does or does not work.

HOW TO WRITE NARRATION

Make a Point: Narration explains. State what you plan to illustrate. Describe the events or steps leading to the point you are describing. Explain the connection between this narrative and the point.

Consider Time: You may begin at the beginning, middle, or end, but once you choose a time-frame, tell the events in sequence. Do not skip around. Decide where to begin by determining what the reader needs to know first. Go on from there.

Choose a Point of View: Managers, programmers, clients, users, and salespeople see events differently. Choose the viewpoint that most accurately and effectively presents the events for your reader. Be consistent once you select the point of view.

Use Relevant Details: Stay on the subject. Tell only the events necessary to understand the point of the narrative.

Be Complete and Precise: Tell all the relevant information you know about the event. Let the reader decide what is important or unimportant. Your duty is to tell the entire sequence so that the reader will understand the event and be able to use the information.

6. Process Analysis

A process analysis explains how something works or describes the individual steps that make something happen. The process may be either manual or mechanical.

Specifications for any computer system are processes that later are programmed and implemented. Good process analysis provides an early understanding of how the system will function. It allows those involved to spot wrongly conceived, impractical, or inaccurate processes. The earlier mistakes are caught, the less costly they are to correct.

HOW TO WRITE A PROCESS ANALYSIS

Have a Purpose: Know what you want to explain. Write to that point. Is it to understand or to reproduce the process?

Be Clear About Your Purpose: Do not confuse process and procedure. A procedure description tells how to do something. It is a set of instructions. A process analysis tells how something works.

Know the Process Inside-out: You cannot explain if you do not understand. Do you know why, when, and where the process is done? The steps necessary to complete it? The right order of those steps? Who does it? What one needs to do it?

Know Your Audience: How much does the reader know? What can you assume? Determine the reader's level of understanding and write to it.

Use Visual Aids If Helpful: A picture is worth a thousand words! Clearly label illustrations.

Example 19

The excerpt from the following program specifications effectively explains the process for solving linear programming problems using the graphical method. The program will become computer-aided instruction for the teaching of linear programming.

PROCESS	SCREENS GENERATED	FUNCTION
4	39–42	The student makes the entries necessary to graph each constraint. The first input entry consists of the coordinates of two points that lie on the equality portion of the constraint. These two points are verified as valid values satisfying the constraint equation. If the point(s) are invalid, the student is asked to repeat entry for the invalid point(s). If the points are valid, then calculations are performed to determine the point(s) where the constraint equation intersects the axes of the graph. The point(s) intersecting the axes are used with the Applesoft HGR graphic commands to draw the equality portion of each constraint.
		For screen 42, the Shape Table is used to generate a crosshair (+) that can be moved around the graph to allow the student to identify the area of inequality. The

PROCESS	SCREENS GENERATED	FUNCTION
		coordinates of the point chosen by the student are verified as valid values satisfying the constraint equation. If the point(s) chosen are incorrect, the student repeats screen 42 and the process of positioning the crosshair (+). When the student correctly identifies the area of inequality, the Applesoft HGR commands are used to shade that area using a striped pattern associating the constraint line with its shading by using the same color for both. This process is repeated for each of the constraints, up to a maximum of five.

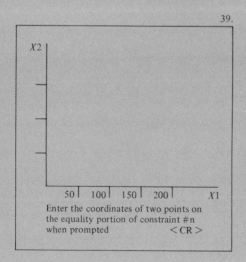

39.

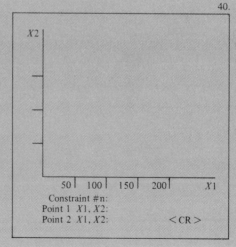

40.

PART ONE INTRODUCTION

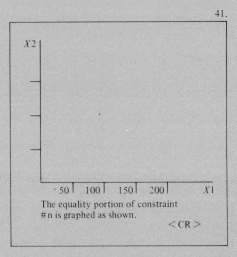

41.

The equality portion of constraint #n is graphed as shown.
<CR>

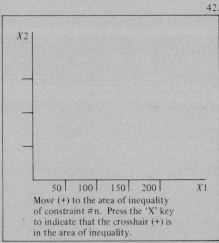

42.

Move (+) to the area of inequality of constraint #n. Press the 'X' key to indicate that the crosshair (+) is in the area of inequality.

COMMENT
This example illustrates a good process analysis:

> The writer understands the purpose (to explain how process 4 works) and understands how, when, and where the process is performed.
> The audience know they must have a background in algebra, computers, and linear programming.
> The clearly labeled visual aids support the explanation.

7. Procedure ✎

A procedure explains how to do something. Two primary documents—user manuals and operations manuals—are made up of procedures. Therefore, you must know how to write clear instructions.

HOW TO WRITE A PROCEDURE

Know Your Audience: Determine what the reader knows. Then you know at what point you can begin.

Write in Sequence: Record the procedure exactly as it is performed. Do not skip actions. Do not assume the user will know how to get from one step to another.

Tell When the Procedure Is Completed: Do not assume the user will know. What signifies that the procedure is finished? Should the user turn the equipment off? Should he or she lock the room? Does the user need to take or send anything to another office? Be complete.

Remember the Following:
1. Tell what material or equipment is needed.
2. Tell how much time is needed to complete the procedure. Indicate lapses between major steps or between steps in a sequence.
3. Explain unfamiliar words.
4. Put warnings where they can be read before mistakes are made.
5. Use transitions. Number steps 1,2,3,etc. Link activities with words like "first," "next," "then," "afterwards," "finally."
6. Write in short sentences or use lists. Do not clutter directions with extra words.

Format: Arrange information so that it is easy to read. Highlight different stages in the procedure by numbering, spacing, underlining, capitalizing, etc.

Test Your Instructions: Have someone unfamiliar with the procedure perform it and give you constructive criticism.

Example 20

This example fails to follow two very simple, but important, rules for writing instructions effectively: parallelism (writing so items correspond in structure, format, etc.) and consistency. A rewrite follows.

Example 20A

```
              Operation Instructions for A101
This job stream is used to select married alumni from the alumni
file.

1. Mount the REMOVE4 disk pack on disk drive 200.
2. Mount a large scratch tape on tape drive 181.
3. Run the A101 job deck into the reader.
4. When the console asks for the date, type the current date in
   the following format: //DATE,05/05/81.
5. After the job has ended, BG WAITING FOR WORK will be dis-
   played on the console. Remove the scratch tape and the
   REMOVE4 disk pack.
6. Print the output on fanfold paper. Lay the printout and job
   deck on the output table.

  *If the job cancels, type in MSG BG and have the system pro-
grammer look at why it cancelled.
```

COMMENT

1. The format is inconsistent. Instructions 1,2,3,4, and 5 give a single instruction; number 6 gives two instructions ("print" and "lay"). Once you begin a pattern do not change it. Readers expect repetition; they would see the first instruction in number 6 and not expect another, so they could miss it. The numbers are not easy to see. Separate numbers from the text.
2. The sentence structure is not parallel. Instructions 1,2,3, and 6 begin with action verbs ("mount," "run," etc.), but instructions 4 and 5 begin with explanatory phrases ("When the . . .," "After the . . ."). Structure all sentences alike.
3. The instruction in item 4 is ambiguous. The "05" is used for both day and month; be clear in instructions.
4. The * has no reference. What number or place in the text does it refer to? Place comments or warnings next to what they relate to.
5. Avoid jargon. "Job stream" is computerese.

3   STRUCTURES FOR WRITING   45

Example 20B

The rewrite addresses the previous criticisms.

> Operating Instructions for A101
>
> This program selects married alumni from the alumni file.
>
> 1. Mount the REMOVE4 disk pack on disk drive 200.
> 2. Mount a large scratch tape on tape drive 181.
> 3. Run the A101 job deck into the reader.
>   Note: If the job cancels, type in MSG BG and have the system programmer look at why it cancelled.
> 4. Type the current date in the following form when the console asks for the date:
>
>   // DATE, 02/31/81
>
> 5. Wait for the comment: BG WAITING FOR WORK.
> 6. Remove the scratch tape and the REMOVE4 disk pack.
> 7. Print the output on fanfold paper.
> 8. Lay the printout and job deck on the output table.

Example 21

This example has some good writing and some problems. See comments afterwards.

> User's Manual for Pharmacy Information System
>
> This system was designed for the inexperienced user. The computer prompts all required user inputs. Menu-driven procedures give the user several options . . . [The following excerpt comes after some comments about the general features of the system.]
>
> PROCEDURE I: SYSTEM START-UP
>
> To start, load the system from the disk and run it as follows. Do this each time the computer is turned on.
>
> 1. Turn on the computer and the monitor.
> 2. Wait for the] symbol to appear.

3. Type LOAD ASTUA and press return.
4. Wait until the red light on the disk drive goes off and the] reappears with the flashing cursor. It will take 45-90 seconds.
5. Type RUN.
6. Enter the date when it is asked for (press return).
7. The menu will appear like this:
   a. create new files
   b. add to an existing file
   c. retrieve a record from a file
   d. change or delete a record
   e. process a prescription
   f. produce an insurance form
   g. update a file
   h. exit

Select your activity by entering the correct number followed by "return." Each activity is described in the following procedures. When the activity is finished, the system will return to the master menu. If an error occurs or the] and flashing cursor appears, you can restart the system by starting at step 2 above.

COMMENT

Good Points
1. The writer identifies and addresses a particular audience ("the inexperienced user").
2. The format uses numbers to separate the instructions, thereby making them easy to read.
3. The instructions appear in sequence.
4. The user knows when the procedure is finished ("When the activity is finished . . .").

Things to Improve
1. An "inexperienced user" will need definitions of "user inputs," "menu driven," and "load the system."
2. Directions for number 1 ("Turn on the computer and the monitor") are not complete. How does one do that?
3. References to press return should be consistent. Number 3 says press return; number 6 has press return in parentheses; the first sentence of the final paragraph mentions only return and has it in quotation marks.
4. The sentence that begins the final paragraph ("Select your activity . . .") appears to be an instruction like the other seven. Make it number 8.

5. Make each instruction complete. Does the user press return in number 5?
6. Terms should be consistent. In number 7, the writer says "menu," but in the final paragraph, the same item is called "master menu."

8. Cause and Effect

A good problem solver can understand and explain why a situation has come about. To explain, you can use cause and effect.

First decide whether the present situation is the cause or the effect of what is happening. To determine the difference, analyze carefully. Is there more than one cause? Does the appearance of cause mean it actually was the cause? When the cause is present, does the effect always follow? You must be equally inquisitive when investigating effect.

HOW TO WRITE USING CAUSE AND EFFECT

Make a Point: Show what has happened; then explain either what caused it to happen or what effects have occurred as a result of its happening.

Structure the Explanation: Identify the cause. List and explain effects. Identify the effect(s). List and explain cause(s).

Example 22

This explanation about solving linear programming problems effectively uses cause and effect.

```
The student inspects and graphical representation of his or her
constraints to determine if the LP problem has a bounded feasi-
ble region.
```

COMMENT

The situation is explained.

```
If the student's answer is incorrect (cause), he or she will be
prompted again (effect). If the feasible region is unbounded
(cause), the process is terminated, and the student is given the
opportunity to work another LP problem (effect).
```

COMMENT

The cause is first identified, then the effect is explained.

✔ 9. Persuasion

To persuade is to write so convincingly that the reader will accept your position. Persuasion's most obvious place in computer system writing is the proposal, but your ability to write opinions so that others accept them is a valuable skill to have and use throughout system development.

HOW TO WRITE USING PERSUASION

Make a Point: Know what you are trying to accomplish. Stay on that subject.

Write Using Good Reasoning: Be a careful thinker. Prepare. Know your facts. Organize your ideas.

Be Fair: Do not twist or misrepresent facts. Be objective. Know your situation well and state it clearly. Facts and figures persuade in the professional world. Know them.

Examples of persuasion appear in the next chapter, "The Proposal."

CHECKLIST: CHAPTER 3
Structure Your Writing

1. DEFINITION
   Use to explain something.
   Know the purpose.
   Know the audience.
   Structure the definition.

2. COMPARISON AND CONSTRAST
   Use to examine two items.
   Make a point.
   Be complete and fair.
   Use the block or point-by-point pattern.

3. CLASSIFICATION AND DIVISION
   Use to examine three or more items.
   Make a point.
   Establish a unifying principle.
   Organize for easy use.

4. DESCRIPTION
   Use to tell what something is, looks like, or does.
   Make a point.
   Begin with a definition.
   Be precise and objective.
   Present information in an orderly manner.

5. NARRATION
   Use to tell a series of closely related happenings.
   Make a point.
   Tell events in sequence.
   Choose a point of view and be consistent.
   Use relevant details.
   Be complete.

6. PROCESS ANALYSIS
   Use to explain how something works.
   Have a purpose.
   Know process inside-out.
   Know the audience.
   Use visual aids.

7. PROCEDURE
   Use to explain how to do something.
   Know the audience.
   Write in sequence.
   Tell when finished.
   Format for easy use.
   Test instructions.

8. CAUSE AND EFFECT
   Use to explain reasons and results.
   Make a point.
   Structure explanation.

9. PERSUASION
   Use to convince reader of your position.
   Make a point.
   Use good reasoning.
   Be fair.

PART TWO

ANALYSIS

Analysis is probably the most important and most difficult work of system development. To analyze, one must observe, read, listen, measure, consider, judge, and conclude. Only people, not computers, can do this work.

Analysis is both a stage in the system development cycle and an activity that permeates the whole cycle. As an activity, it is one people continually do. They write programs, determine audiences, consider cost-effectiveness, solve problems, judge a system's effectiveness, or do other work of creating, implementing, and maintaining a computer system. This activity is not limited to any one position. It is important to be a good thinker and a good problem solver whether one is literally a systems analyst, or a client, finance officer, project manager, production person, software developer, or anyone else who must judge the effectiveness of the system's performance and its documentation at any given point.

Analysis is also the formal stage of system development that we will address in Part Two. In the analysis stage, the system to be created is defined and its specifications are declared. Unfortunately, good analysis cannot guarantee a good system. Too many other factors are involved: a community of users, the availability and accuracy of information, time, money, and equipment. In spite of this, it is important to analyze correctly.

We shall study two documents common to the analysis stage of system documentation: *the proposal* and the *functional specification*. Each document is defined, then examples and comments follow which let you evaluate documentation and lead you to understand what makes effective writing.

4

The Proposal I

What Is a Proposal and What Is Its Function?

A proposal puts forth an idea. In the professional world, that "idea" is traditionally a bid for work, so in one way, writing a proposal is like entering a contest. The proposal is your completed entry blank; the client or management is the judge; and company time and money are the prize. As in most contests, no second chance is given. Competition is keen and competitors are astute.

The fact that a proposal is a competitive document does not make it a game. Writing the proposal is a very serious activity, for through it your company acquires work. Your ability to write a successful proposal or to judge a proposal's chance of success is vital both to the company's well-being and to your personal success with that company.

The bid does not always take the form of a formal report. Often a project is begun as a result of a conversation between two people; one agrees to see if a data processing solution can be worked out to serve the other's needs. Other projects start from simple requests written in memoranda. Informal proposals are adequate, even proper, for small or simple projects. They serve the purpose and save time and money.

A large, complicated project, however, requires a more formal document. It is known by several names: the conceptual design, the problem definition, the feasibility study, or the proposal—the name we shall use. All of these reports define a problem, state a solution, and discuss its benefits and cost. All have the same purpose, to present information so that management can decide whether to go forward with the project. Your object is to persuade, and to do that your proposal must be as precise and reliable as a good report and as convincing as a good sales pitch.

The proposal is a prime document. It is first in time or order, and it must be first quality.

The proposal does more than just initiate the documentation cycle; it prepares or "primes" the cycle for what follows. Without the proposal, nothing could follow: no analysis, no design, no implementation.

In like manner, the proposal does more than act as a "starter." Information contained in the proposal becomes the foundation for building the system. Therefore, the quality of the analysis in this first document directly affects the soundness and stability of the system.

Who Writes Proposals?

System analysts and designers write proposals regularly. But often programmers, operations people, and others involved in collecting information become involved in writing the proposal. If the project becomes a team effort, it is a good idea to have one person act as "editor" to ensure that the entire report is consistent in format and style.

People other than writers can also contribute. For example, a person's remarks made during one of the planning sessions can become part of the text; someone else may provide pieces of written information, others may read drafts of the work and make suggestions. Each person who prepares, writes, or evaluates the proposal can approach the document in the structured manner suggested in this chapter.

Who Reads Proposals?

Many people read the proposal as it comes into being and after it becomes a formal document. But not all of these are the formal audience for the proposal. As you write, you should keep in mind the proposal's formal audience and not be distracted by those readers who are not part of it.

Organize and Outline

A parts list for constructing a traditional proposal follows. It is not necessary to use every part for every proposal, nor is it necessary to write the proposal using these parts in this order. What is required is that your proposal interrelate all of the parts you choose to use and that you decide what parts you need and what order is best for your particular writing task:

1. A statement of the problem and an explanation of its relation to current operations
2. A statement of the proposed solution and its scope
3. Operational requirements of proposed system
4. Operating environment of proposed system
5. Benefits
6. Budget or costs or both
7. Implementation plan
8. Evaluation
9. Alternatives considered

These parts are also useful if you are a critic. An effective proposal should cover these points.

Practice in Writing and Evaluating

Good writers are good readers who can read their work as their critics will. This insight allows them to evaluate their writing problems and revise the text accordingly.

Good critics must have the same ability; only their task is to tell others how to rewrite.

THE WALKTHROUGH

A structured approach to system design and analysis uses an evaluation tool called a "walkthrough." Whether the walkthrough is conducted informally or formally, it causes everyone involved in creating the system to "play computer" with others who review the work. The group takes a step-by-step "walk" through the code or part that is being evaluated.

Others in the organization bring a fresh viewpoint or objective response, so they are able to spot errors and make suggestions that solve problems.

THE TALKTHROUGH

The "talkthrough," a new evaluation tool, is similar to a walkthrough, but performed differently. Instead of having someone else join us in reviewing our documentation, we are going to learn to be creator, examiner, writer, and critic. Our goal is to be objective, to spot ineffective writing, and revise.

PART TWO   ANALYSIS

CHECKLIST: CHAPTER 4
The Proposal I

1.	DEFINITION	A bid for work.
2.	FUNCTION	Defines a problem and states a solution. Persuades a reader to accept the proposed solution.
3.	WRITER	System analyst and system designer.
4.	AUDIENCE	Client.

5

The Proposal II

Parts of the Proposal

1. Statement of Problem and Relation ✔ of Problem to Current Operations

Begin this section by answering:

    What is the problem?
    Why is it a problem?
    Why is the problem important?
    What is already known and documented about the problem?

    Write forcefully, but carefully. Do not overstate the problem and cause the reader to label you a "Chicken Little"—someone who runs around crying out that something terrible is happening when in fact it is not. Chicken Little lost her credibility; you must not lose yours.
    One effective way to organize this section is to use the pattern of cause and effect:

    State effect: the problem(s)
    List cause(s): current operations
    Develop each cause: establish causal relation of operation causing problem.

As in most cause-and-effect analysis, the challenge is to avoid assumptions. Do not mistake appearance for reality. What appears to be the cause or the problem, or what someone says is the cause or problem, may in fact not be so. Do your own careful investigation. Ask questions. Observe. Make your own conclusions. Be able to support them.

If you find that the problem is caused not by current operations but by outside factors, say so. In some cases, you may even decide that it is impractical to use the computer to solve the problem. Either discovery may cancel the need for further discussion or may introduce a new project. What is important is to analyze well and report correctly.

2. Scope and Statement of Proposed Solution

The fit of Section 2 to Section 1 must be like tongue and groove. Whatever the problem, the solution must address it comprehensively. If the problem is four-fold, the solution must solve each part of the problem or at least acknowledge the part not solved and explain why this part remains unsolved. Format the information so it clearly matches and responds to the problem.

You define the scope of the system as you mark functions of the current operation to be changed or eliminated. Remember the proposal is an introductory document; do not tell the whole history of the solution. If the proposed solution is adopted, there will be time later to go into details.

EXAMPLES FOR SECTIONS 1 AND 2: PROBLEM AND ITS RELATION TO CURRENT OPERATION/SOLUTION STATEMENT

Example 23

Imagine a colleague has given you the following statement to read and has asked you to comment on its effectiveness. Jot down some constructive comments that would improve this writing. Use both the ideas of Chapter 2 and the discussion of the role of the proposal as a basis for your criticisms.

PROPOSED: A Microfiche System to Ease Printer Burden

CURRENT OPERATIONAL PROBLEM

(1) Recently, Company A bought Company B and assumed their data processing needs. Before this merger, our output facilities were being used 70%. Our three IBM 3203 printers were operating 16 hours each day for a total output of 60,481 pages per day. The 70% utilization factor left ample room for the growth and development of this corporation without modification to our hardware configuration. We had the capacity to meet our 8 A.M. deadline with one printer down.

(2) The added responsibility of Company B's work has not seriously affected our CPU utilization, however, our printer utilization has increased to 95%. If one of our printers is down

for more than 2 hours, it is impossible to meet our deadline. A slight surge in the quantity of our reports can also cause us to miss our deadline. When operating at 95% of our printing capacity, ample resources to handle corporate growth and expansion are not available.

(3) Researching ways to ease our problem, we discovered that our user departments are running out of report storage space. Some reports must be kept for one month, and others, like government reports, must be kept for seven years. The acquisition of Company B has compounded the problem.

PROPOSED SOLUTION

(4) Company A has two alternatives to ease the printer utilization percentage. The obvious solution is to rent another printer. Our present system can have another printer added with no channel modifications. However, it would take two to three months for IBM to order and install the additional printer. New equipment requires modification to the supervisor program. A system programmer would need approximately 4 hours to modify and implement the new supervisor program. This alternative would solve the operations department's problem, but would do nothing to ease the user departments' problems.

(5) The second alternative for Company A is the use of Computer Output Microfilm (COM). This alternative will solve the operations department's problem as well as the user departments' storage problems. Each piece produced by COM is known as a microfiche, a $4\frac{1}{8} \times 5\frac{3}{4}$ inch piece of clear plastic which contains the reduced images of what would have been 207 pages of computer output plus an index frame. A COM system would require two new pieces of equipment, a recorder and a duplicator; but it would not have any effect on the hardware or software of the host system.

(6) Several companies market microfiche equipment in this area. Any of these companies can have a recorder and duplicator installed and functioning within one month.

COMMENT

I gave myself the same assignment and came up with the following ideas. Compare your comments with mine. We may differ. That is fine as long as we both spot instances of weak writing and tell the writer how to improve.

General Comment

1. *Problems/Solutions:* Restructure and rewrite the proposal so that solutions are offered to stated problems. As is, this writing is not effective

because it rambles and crosses back on itself. See comments in following text for suggested reorganization and rewording.
2. *Audience:* The writer assumes all readers will understand in-house language; if this is true, fine. If not, I have noted examples of language that need explaining.
3. *Organize/Outline:* Reorganize for effective paragraphing; group related ideas; improve overall effectiveness. See notes in following text.
4. *Format:* A comparison/constrast pattern for the solution will aid understanding. See text.
5. *Be Responsible for What You Write:* Explain source of percentages.

Specific Comments Attached to Text

PROPOSED: A Microfiche System to Ease Printer Burden

CURRENT OPERATIONAL PROBLEM

(1) Recently, Company A bought Company B and assumed their data processing needs.

COMMENT
Give specific date of purchase. Give full company names and locations.

Before this merger, our **output** facilities were being used 70%.

COMMENT
Is "merger" accurate or is it an acquisition? "Our" is indefinite. Does it mean Company A's? Say so. Is "output facilities" in-house language or jargon? What does it precisely mean? How was the figure 70% arrived at? Give the source of this figure.

Our three IBM 3203 **printers** were operating 16 hours each day for a total **output** of 60,481 pages per day. The **70%** utilization factor left ample room for the growth and development of this corporation without modification to our hardware configuration.

COMMENT
Simplify language. "60,481" is unneeded precision; it confuses. Say "over 60,000 pages."
 The phrase "70% utilization factor" is stilted language; "hardware configuration" is pompous language. Does that mean printers?

We had the capacity to meet our 8 A.M. deadline with one printer down.

COMMENT
Reorganize so like ideas are together. Notice the words in boldface. The writer first mentions "output"—then "70%"—then "printers"—then "output"—then "70%." Put everything about output together, about 70% together, about printers together.

Rewrite: Before this acquisition, Company A printed over 60,000 pages per day which is approximately 70% of the company's printing capacity. The company's three IBM 3203 printers, operating 16 hours a day, adequately processed the printing and consistently delivered the work in time to meet the daily 8 A.M. deadline. This deadline could be met even with one printer down.

```
    (2) The added responsibility of Company B's work has not
seriously affected our CPU utilization; however, our printer
utilization has increased to 95%.
```

COMMENT
Poor organization. Put like ideas together. Paragraph 2 begins talking about "CPU's." After that one sentence, the writer goes back to "printers," the topic of paragraph (1). Move the CPU part of the sentence somewhere else or eliminate it. If it is used, tell what a "CPU" is. Not all readers will know. Begin paragraph (2). "The added responsibility of Company B's work increases the printer use to 95%." Now the writer is continuing to write about printers and the informations flows and relates. Make clear that the *effect* of including Company B's output is the *cause* of the printer's use being increased to 95%.

```
If one of our printers is down for more than 2 hours, it is im-
possible to meet our deadline. A slight surge in the quantity of
our reports can also cause us to miss our deadline. When operat-
ing at 95% of our printing capacity, ample resources to handle
corporate growth and expansion are not available.
```

COMMENT
Rewrite to show three problems resulting from the increased demand on the company's printers:

EFFECT	PROBLEM
1. Miss deadline	If breakdown, no backup printer
2. Miss deadline	If printing increases, no extra printer for overload
3. Unable to expand	Equipment not available to accept new work

(3) Researching ways to ease our problem, we discovered that our user departments are running out of report storage space. Some reports must be kept for one month while the government reports must be kept for seven years. The acquisition of Company B has compounded the problem.

COMMENT
Rewrite this paragraph to match the organization of paragraphs (1) and (2). Talk of Company A's situation before and after buying Company B. First, state Company A's upcoming storage problem before it acquired Company B; then tell how that problem is magnified by adding Company B.

PROPOSED SOLUTION

(4) Company A has two alternatives to ease the printer utilization percentage. The obvious solution is to rent another printer. Our present system can have another printer added with no channel modifications. However, it would take two to three months for IBM to order and install the additional printer. New equipment requires modification to the supervisor program. A system programmer would need approximately 4 hours to modify and implement the new supervisor program. This alternative would solve the operations department's problem, but would do nothing to ease the user departments' problems.

(5) The second alternative for Company A is the use of Computer Output Microfilm (COM). This alternative will solve the operations department's problem as well as the user departments' storage problems. Each piece produced by COM is known as a microfiche, a $4\frac{1}{8} \times 5\frac{3}{4}$ inch piece of clear plastic which contains the reduced images of what would have been 207 pages of computer output plus an index frame. A COM system would require two new pieces of equipment, a recorder and a duplicator; but it would not have any effect on the hardware or software of the host system.

COMMENT
Format paragraphs (4) and (5) differently. Begin by stating two alternatives. Then list comparative information so that it is easy to read and compare.

Example
1. Renting Another Printer
   Advantages
   _____
   _____

Disadvantages

_____

_____

2. Buying Computer Output Microfilm (COM)
   Advantages

   _____

   _____

   Disadvantages

   _____

   _____

Note: Each alternative must cover effect of 1. deadline, 2. expansion, 3. storage.

Write clearly. In the statement "Company A has two alternatives...," it is not clear what they are. Later, the writer speaks of "new equipment." Is that the "rented printer," or does this refer to the second alternative?

(6) Several companies market microfiche equipment in this area. Any of these companies can have a recorder and duplicator installed and functioning within one month.

COMMENT
Paragraph error: A new paragraph is not needed since this information is still on COM. You normally begin a new paragraph whenever you begin a new subject.

Example 24

Read the following problem statement and the problem's relation to current operations. Numbers appear throughout the text where I think writing problems exist. Decide what you think the problem is. My comments appear afterwards, so you can compare. Again, we do not have to match. The important thing is to develop a critical sense, spot writing problems, and consider how to correct them.

(1)

The Safety Incentive Awards Program at C.M. & J. **(2)** Chemical Company **(3)** awards points **(4)** to employees for accident-free periods of time. **(5)** These safety points are subsequently used by employees **(6)** to claim awards. **(7)** Presently, all record keeping

64 PART TWO ANALYSIS

is done manually **(8)** at an estimated time **(9)** of eight hours per month. This time is spent updating **(10)** the employee's points-file, **(11)** issuing certificates for penalty points, and issuing certificates for monthly safety awards. In addition, certificates are issued **(12)** for bonus points which are awarded at six-month intervals to employees who have not had an accident within that six-month **(13)** time period. **(14)** The Data Processing Department has decided **(15)** that an automated system could reduce the personnel time required for administration of the system **(16)** and improve the accuracy of the system **(17)**.

COMMENT
1. Label the section. Headings should separate sections in the text.
2. The first time a writer cites a company that is known by its initials, state the full name and put the initials in parentheses following the name. Afterwards, one may use just initials.
3. Where is the company located?
4. The "Program" cannot award "points." Be accurate. The company awards points through the program.
5. How long is a "period of time"? WHAT IS THE PROBLEM? I should have an idea by now. I do not.
6. How are the points used? Which employees use them?
7. This whole sentence is confusing to me. What does "for various numbers of points" mean? What awards? I STILL DO NOT KNOW THE PROBLEM.
8. "Manually" by whom? How many people are involved? How is the process manually performed?
9. Who estimated the time? How was the estimate determined?
10. Is the time well-spent? How is the "updating" done? Who spends this time?
11. Grammar: Change "employees's" to "employees'" (plural possessive) and "points-file" to "point-files." The plurals are needed to match the plurals (certificates) in the remaining part of the sentence.
12. The transition is meaningless—"in addition" to what? Actually, the information in this sentence needs to be included as the fourth item in the previous sentence. Add another item to the "issuing" list: "This time is spent updating . . . issuing certificates for penalty points, for monthly safety awards, and for bonus points which are awarded. . . ."
13. Unnecessary to repeat "six-month."
14. WHAT IS THE PROBLEM? I STILL DO NOT KNOW.
15. Did the Data Processing Department take it upon itself to "decide?" Is it that department's responsibility to decide such things? Who in the department decided this? What was the reason for deciding this?

16. Is there a problem with the "personnel time?" If so, I do not know what it is. If this is the Problem Statement, it is a poor one.
17. I did not know there was "inaccuracy." Is this part of the problem? How or why is it a problem?

SUMMARY COMMENT
The fact that most comments became questions indicates that the writer needs to inform better. Remember, the writer must decide what the reader does not know and what he or she needs to know. Furthermore, the writer must show the connection between current operations and the problem, between cause and effect. It is not up to the reader to figure it out.

Example 25

Read the following sample. Use the form that follows the sample to structure your analysis.

Problem Definition

Each time a weaver envisions a pattern for a piece of cloth, the actual weaving must be delayed until the weaver completes preliminary tasks.

Through interviews with Ms. Jane Doe, user, Department of Fine Arts, University of Evansville, Evansville, IN, the following problems were cited within the "preludes to weaving":

Problems with manual drafting of patterns:
　1. Causes time-consuming design methods
　2. Lacks ease of modification to pattern draft

Problems with calculations of yarn quantities:
　1. Causes mathematical computations to be tedious
　2. Lacks ease of adaptation to change in loom types

Consequently, a need exists to design a system with a degree of versatility to adapt to the unique needs of weavers.

RELATIONSHIP OF PROBLEM TO CURRENT OPERATIONS

A weaver uses graph paper and colored pencils to draw a pattern draft:

　1. Mental adjustments must be made between the graph paper weave and the size of the cloth weave.

PART TWO   ANALYSIS

2. Changes made to the perceived pattern design usually result in the redrawing of the entire draft.
3. Change in yarn texture or color can result in a redraw of the entire draft.

The amount of yarn needed for a project depends upon several variables:

1. Changes in yarn density or pattern design require new calculations of the quantity.
2. Variations in the number of harnesses on a loom affect the quantities of yarn calculated.
3. Size of the reed affects the yarn quantity calculated.

PROPOSED SOLUTION TO THE PROBLEM

The proposed system, *Preludes to Weaving*, demonstrates the following characteristics:

1. Versatility: The system has a wide variety of features available to the user.
2. Modifiability: The system can easily be altered to adjust to the changing needs of the user.
3. Adaptability: The system has the ability to adjust to the various loom specifications.

The proposed system meets the following requirements:

1. Provides the ability to duplicate actual cloth weave size in the pattern design
2. Facilitates changes made to the pattern during drafting
3. Reduces time required to draw the three drafts required for each pattern design:
   a. weave draft
   b. warp plan (threading draft)
   c. chain draft
4. Simplifies yarn quantity calculations
5. Provides methods converting the drafts and yarn quantities for use on various looms

SYSTEM SCOPE

The *Preludes to Weaving System* replaces the manual methods used to perform preliminary tasks:

1. The CRT screens direct the user through the use of graphics

for pattern design drafting and through the calculations for the yarn quantities.
2. A file stores the many different yarn textures and densities. This file provides the information needed in calculations of the yarn quantities needed for a project.
3. A loom specification file contains the information concerning the quantity of harnesses on a particular loom for use in yarn calculations.
4. Additional calculations available to the user include:
   a. warp length
   b. reed size
   c. weft density
   d. number of warp ends
   e. proportion of weft to warp
5. A printer provides a report of the calculations.

Evaluation Guide
1. Do you know the *problem*? What is effective or ineffective about the way it is stated?
2. Who is the *audience*? How do you know the writer has an audience in mind? How consistent is the tone?
3. How *well-organized* is this sample? What writing techniques make it organized or unorganized?
4. How effective is the *format*? What does the writer do to make a good appearance?
5. Is the *language* of the document clear and appropriate? Why do you say it is or is not?
6. How well does the "proposed solution" answer the "problem"? Why is it easy or difficult to see the relationship?
7. What *additional comments* or *suggestions* can you make?

SUMMARY COMMENT
This problem/proposed solution statement seems well-written, clearly organized, clearly presented, carefully thought out, and, in general, very effective. The problem seems real and the solution seems practical.

3. Operational Requirements of Proposed System

Without going into specifics, describe the proposed operational procedures for machine and manual operations. The reader of the proposal must understand what the proposed solution means in terms of work loads, personnel, procedures, and results.

State the broad objectives the new system is to achieve. Then, clarify the input and output required to meet the objectives:

What information is to be passed in and out of the system?
What form does the input take? How often is it submitted?
How is the input retained?
What form does the output take? How often is it passed out?
What interface does the user have with the input and output?

Remember your audience! Most likely you are not writing to another computer specialist. Explain terms like "fields" and "files" and "online," etc. If the reader must decide upon the feasibility of your proposal from reading this report, write clearly. Help the person understand the information.

4. Operating Environment of Proposed System

Is the data collected online or offline? Depending upon the collection method, identify equipment needs: card readers, terminals, etc. How many of each is needed? Where will each be placed?

What hardware and software is required? Is the software something that is standard, on the market, easily purchasable, or must the software be customized?

EXAMPLES FOR SECTIONS 3 AND 4: OPERATIONAL REQUIREMENTS AND OPERATING ENVIRONMENT OF PROPOSED SYSTEM

Example 26

How do you evaluate this statement of operational requirements?

Operational Requirements:

The requirements to implement this new system would be CRTs, drivers, a table, operating system updates, extra long-term storage, the research team, monthly file backups, a very minimal amount of training.

COMMENT

I cannot make decisions based upon this statement. No specifics are given. How many of anything are needed? Where are they needed? I may not be a computer person; therefore, what are "drivers?" I may know only people who "drive." Eliminate unnecessary words like "extra" (long-term . . .) and "very" (minimal . . .). Computer documentation should be crisp.

Example 27

A computer facility is converting from a card input environment to an online environment. A telecommunication software package is needed. The requirements for selecting such a package follow. How effectively are they stated?

OPERATIONAL REQUIREMENTS:

Hardware Requirements:
1. The package must be compatible with:
   a. IBM 4331
   b. DOS VS/E operating system
   c. CICS (Customer Information Control System)
2. The package must require no more than 10% additional memory.

Software Requirements:
1. The package must support up to 50 terminals.
2. The package must allow for conversion to an interactive programming environment.
3. The package must have a response time of under two seconds at peak usage.
4. The package must be user friendly.
5. The package must contain:
   a. A full screen editor
   b. File maintenance and protection facilities
   c. A built-in utility macros

COMMENT
The reader is obviously someone who understands computers. Given this, the information is specific. The format is effective.

5. Benefits ✓

Any change is troublesome and time consuming. To have people agree to change, the benefits in cost savings and productivity must be clear. Format the information so it is easy to read. Use lists, charts, comparison and contrast, or anything else that visually organizes the information.

EXAMPLES FOR SECTION 5: BENEFITS

Example 28

The following example should be reorganized to be more effective. Decide how you would redesign it. Outline your design on your own paper and compare it to mine that follows. In Example 29, I address other writing problems in this writing sample.

Proposal to Replace Punched Card System with
CRT Terminal System

Benefits:

The benefits to be derived from the new CRT system would be so numerous and varied that I have chosen to list them:

1. Substantial monetary savings, due to cheapness and dependability of CRTs and elimination of cards.
2. Increased user response speed.
3. Greater space utilization, as CRTs are smaller than keypunches, and card readers would not be required.
4. More consistent usability, since CRTs do not break down nearly as often as mechanical keypunches.
5. Convenience, since students would not need to bring in their punched cards to run their programs.
6. Easier editing.
7. Users can get immediate response to many queries right at the terminal.
8. Students will gain experience in operating modern equipment, that which is rapidly replacing card systems.
9. CRTs make less noise than keypunches.
10. Expandability and flexibility, since technology is making rapid progress in this field.
11. The need to stand in two lines, one for a keypunch and one for a card reader, would be eliminated.

As you can see, the benefits of a CRT system are almost overwhelming.

COMMENT

The list attempts to show how a CRT system is superior to a punched card system. That means it compares and contrasts. The writer should use the comparison/contrast pattern to organize. The writer does not. Sometimes the list mentions both the CRT and cards. Other times only one of the two is mentioned. Sometimes neither is mentioned; instead a benefit is cited. The writing is inconsistent and therefore ineffective. I suggest a chart and give two examples.

A. *Miscellaneous List*

ITEM OF COMPARISON	KEYPUNCH	CRT
1. Cost saving	requires cards	uses no cards
2. Maintenance	prone to breakdown	reliable performance record
3. Response time	wait till cards punched	immediate/online
4. (item)	(comment)	(comment)

Another way to organize is to group benefits. This pattern is particularly effective when you wish to emphasize. For example, the administration reviewing this proposal may think that serving the students is a number one priority. If your writing shows that the student user is better served by the proposed system, your organization makes it easy for the reader to see what will cause him or her to approve the system.

B. *Discriminate List*

ITEM OF COMPARISON	KEYPUNCH	CRT
User Benefits:		
1. Response Time	Students must wait for cards to be punched.	Students have immediate response online.
2. Experience	Students learn on outdated equipment.	Students work on modern equipment.
3. Time saving	Students use two processes to run the programs: keypunch and card reader.	Students use one process to run the program: printing.
Cost Benefits:		
1. (item)	(comment)	(comment)
Maintenance Benefits:		
1. (item)	(comment)	(comment)

Example 29

Example 28 is also written poorly. In this reprint of the example, I have marked language, grammar, and content problems.

Benefits:

The benefits ~~to be derived~~ from the new CRT system ~~would be so~~ *are*] **Wordy**

numerous and varied. ~~that I have chosen to list them:~~

What does "substantial" mean? Be precise.

1. (Substantial) monetary savings, due to (cheapness) and
   omit comma → *CRT's are "cheap"?*
   dependability of (CRTs) and elimination of cards. *Does that mean trash? Poor tone.*

PART TWO   ANALYSIS

> 2. Increased user response speed.
>
> 3. (Greater) space utilization, as CRTs (are smaller) than keypunches, and card readers (would not be required).
>
> 4. (More) consistant usability since CRTs do not break down (nearly) as often as mechanical keypunches.
>
> 5. Convenience, since students would not need to bring in their punched cards to run their programs.
>
> 6. Easier editing.
>
> 7. Users ~~can~~ get immediate response to many queries ~~right~~ at the terminal.
>
> 8. Students ~~will~~ gain experience in operating modern equipment, (~~that which is~~ rapidly replacing card system).
>
> 9. CRTs make less noise than keypunches. *awkward*
>
> 10. Expandability and flexability, since technology is making rapid progress in this field.
>
> 11. (The need to stand in two lines), one for a keypunch and one for a card reader, would be eliminated.
>
> As you can see, the benefits of a CRT system are (almost overwhelming.) *poor business language and tone.*

Annotations:
- *What do these words mean? How much "greater"? How much "more"? How often is "nearly"?*
- *omit comma*
- *Shift in tense. Write in one tense: "are smaller" and "are not required" or "would be smaller" and "would not be required"*
- *what expands and is flexible?*
- *Who needs to stand in line?*
- *Is this a benefit? Reader expects it to be since other ideas begin with a benefit*

COMMENTS

Write the list so all eleven items are alike. As is, the structure is mixed. For instance:

    Number 7 is a sentence; number 10 is a phrase.

    Number 2 and number 6 give a characteristic without identifying whether it belongs to a CRT or to a keypunch; number 3 and number 4 mention both a CRT and a keypunch; number 9 mentions only a CRT; number 7 mentions neither.

Number 7 begins by speaking of the "user." Number 9 begins by speaking of the "CRT." Number 5 begins by speaking of a benefit, "convenience." Begin alike.

The mix of structure makes the list useless because the reader is unable to compare.

Example 30

The following is a benefit sheet for a proposal suggesting a user access security system for the present Data Processing Department at X University. Read the example and decide what you like about it and what you would change.

```
I.  BENEFITS
A.  USER BENEFITS                      WITH IMPLEMENTATION OF
    UNDER CURRENT OPERATIONS           PROPOSED SYSTEM

1.  Users are not aware of the     1.  Users will realize capa-
    full system capabilities           bilities of the system be-
    available in software and          cause the development of
    data.                              authorization tables
                                       will ultimately upgrade
                                       documentation and pro-
                                       vide information on all
                                       software and data ac-
                                       cessible by the user.

2.  A user cannot protect his      2.  The user will be able to
    programs or data from              protect his programs and
    being deleted or cor-              data (by using commands
    rupted because other us-           such as Read Only, Write
    ers can access them.               Only, Execute Only) to
                                       identify those users who
                                       may access the informa-
                                       tion and to identify the
                                       type of sharing allowed.

B.  COMPANY BENEFITS                   WITH IMPLEMENTATION OF
    UNDER CURRENT OPERATIONS           PROPOSED SYSTEM

1.  No means is available to       1.  Users are monitored to
    determine how much time            create a list-log of us-
    users spend on the com-            ers. Their activities and
    puter.                             length of transaction
```

2. The company is open to destruction of vital operating systems, including payroll, customer billing, and inventory control, all of which could be costly or even fatal to the company.
3. The company is subject to industrial espionage because private commercial data such as company secrets and prospects cannot be kept from user access.

will enable the company to make decisions on allocating money to the appropriate departments for DP usage.
2. The operating systems will be protected from destruction and modification by unauthorized users.
3. All priority information will be unavailable to the common user and can be obtained only after proper clearance and identification is made.

COMMENT

Good Points: I like the format. The information is persuasive.

Things to Consider: For efficiency, change complete sentences to phrases or shorter sentences.

REWRITE

B. COMPANY BENEFITS
UNDER CURRENT OPERATIONS

WITH IMPLEMENTATION OF PROPOSED SYSTEM

1. No means to determine time users spend on the computer.

1. Create user-log to note type of activity and length of transaction. Use log to appropriately allocate money to DP departments that most use and need data processing.

Example 31

The following example uses pictures to communicate. How do you judge the effectiveness?

BENEFITS

The following graph depicts the cost benefits of a microfiche system versus our current paper operations.

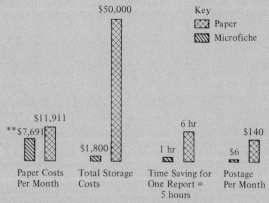

**Cost includes paper used along with microfiche.

COMMENT

I like this presentation but wish the writer had given a source for the microfiche graphs. I assume the "paper" figures are the company's figures. But what about the microfiche figures? The comparison needs to be based on a like company in order to make the information reliable. A "source statement" preceding the graph could take care of this problem.

6. Budget/Costs ✓

Budgets are always difficult to project. But if you want your project approved, you must estimate the costs and cost savings so the reader can make an informed decision to accept this project. Force yourself to be realistic. Do not underprice, hoping that low costs will make the project attractive. Think of every cost:

    Personnel
    Analyst, programmer, computer time
    Equipment: hardware and software
    Relocation or need for additional space
    New forms—their development and production

    Justify each item in simple, complete terms. Explain your figures. Give sources.
    Format the budget-sheet so the reader understands costs and cost savings. Show the difference between continuing work in the current manner and doing the work in the proposed manner.

PART TWO ANALYSIS

EXAMPLES FOR SECTION 6: BUDGET/COSTS

Two examples of budget costs sheets follow presenting different ways to organize. Consider each for format, clarity, and completeness. What do you want to imitate? What improvements can you suggest?

Example 32

BUDGET: Implementation of a Microfiche System

The following equipment is needed for the implementation of a microfiche system. The machinery will be purchased through a five-year lease with the option to buy.

Initial Costs:
  Initial Costs (first month only)
Fireproof safe	$1,800.00	
Form slides 2 @ $200.00	400.00	
Freight in/out	1,400.00	
Total initial costs		$3,600.00

Monthly Costs:
Processor	$3,250.00	
Maintenance on processor	(In lease)	
Duplicator	660.00	
Maintenance on duplicator	(In lease)	
Monthly total equipment costs		$3,910.00
Processor film (silver) using volume of 6,600/month	$1,179.75	
Chemicals for 5 changes/month @$38.19 per case	190.95	
Duplicating film using volume of 36,000/month @$66.80 per 1,000 feet	1,202.40	
Sales tax	259.32	
Monthly total supply costs		$2,832.42
Total monthly costs		$6,743.42

Revenue Savings:
  Postage to Knoxville per month, $ 134.00
    @$35.00 for 5 reports versus
    $1.50 for 5 microfiche reports
    resulting saving
  Paper saving per month   4,300.00
  Construction costs amortized   833.33
    over 5 years
  Revenue of processing for other   2,800.00
    companies @$35.00 a week for 20
    companies

  Total revenue/saving per month $8,067.33

  Saving $8,067.33
  Costs   6,742.42

  PROFIT per month (excluding $1,324.91
    initial costs)

Example 33

This budget projects the costs of developing a language evaluation manual to be used by consultants who help business people select appropriate data processing languages.

PROJECTED SAVINGS

CURRENT WORKLOAD	PROPOSED WORKLOAD
20 consultants	16 consultants
$25.00 per hour	$25.00 per hour
35 clients per year on the average	44 clients per year on the average
$1,000.00 per client	$800.00 per client

PART TWO ANALYSIS

```
      20 consultants              16 consultants
    × 52 weeks per year          × 52 weeks per year
    × $1,000.00 per week         × $1,000.00 per week
    ─────────────────────        ─────────────────────
    $1,040,000.00 per year       $832,000.00 per year


                        $1,040,000.00
                    −      843,000.00
                        ─────────────
    Annual Savings   $    208,000.00
```

COMMENT

Both examples illustrate thoughtful organization. The way you place words or other information on the page will either help or hinder your effort to write well. In business, time is money. Save your reader time by writing so that the information is understood quickly.

The underlining in Example 32 is most effective; it causes one to see the important figures quickly.

7. Implementation Plan

Design a chart to show when each stage of the system will be designed and implemented. In order to plan well, managers must know when things are to occur.

EXAMPLES FOR SECTION 7: IMPLEMENTATION PLAN

Many different patterns are available for showing your implementation schedule. Three examples follow. My comments precede each example. You may have other suggestions.

Example 34

This chart looks impressive, but I do not know any dates, or how long anything takes, or who does what. I have written the chart to answer some of the questions and to make each statement begin with a verb.

5 THE PROPOSAL II

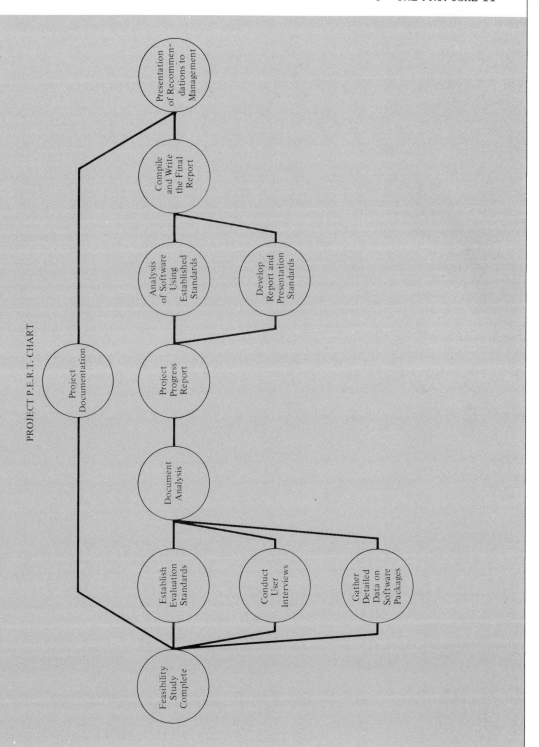

PART TWO ANALYSIS

Example 34a (Rewrite)

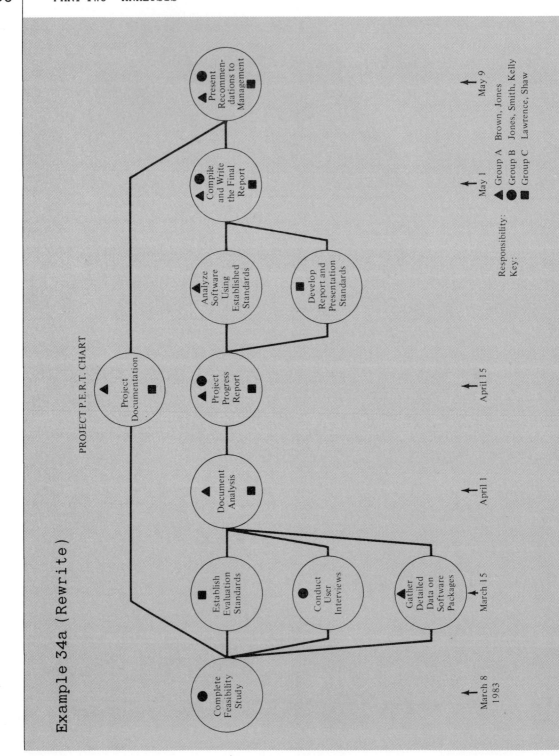

Example 35

The block method is good, but in this example, I cannot determine time. The numbers at the bottom of the sheet do not work. The chart says the numbers mean "Time in months," but it is difficult to determine weeks or know when months begin or end. To revise, replace vertical lines to show weeks and months and use shading to clarify. See Example 35A.

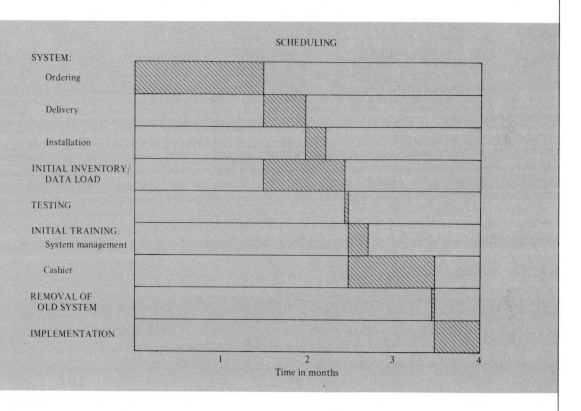

Example 35A (Rewrite)

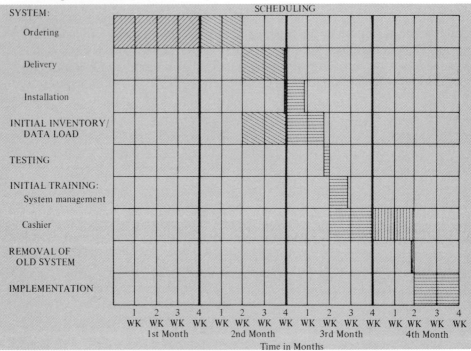

Example 36

Do not design charts with the writing going in two directions. In this example, whichever way readers turn the chart, they can read only part of the information. In the revision, all the information can be read by holding the chart one way. The information is also now more complete.

IMPLEMENTATION PLAN

CONSULTANTS			DATES							
	1/3-15/83	1/16		1/24	1/25	1/26	1/28	1/29	2/2	2/4
1	GATHERING OF INFORMATION	FORMS ANALYSIS SYSTEMS ENHANCEMENTS		STATUS REPORT DUE	FIRST DRAFT DUE	EDITING OF FIRST DRAFT	SECOND DRAFT DUE	EDITING OF SECOND DRAFT	TYPING OF MANUAL	COMPLETED PROJECT
2		FILE ANALYSIS MEMORY ANALYSIS								
3		HARDWARE DEFINITION APPLICATIONS								
4		SOFTWARE DEFINITION COST/BENEFIT ANALYSIS								

5   THE PROPOSAL II

Example 36A (Rewrite)

DATA TECH'S AUDITING SYSTEM'S IMPLEMENTATION PLAN
1/3/83-2/4/83

Plan Designer: Bob Brown
Date of Design: 12/15/83

Consultants	DATES									
	1/3-1/15	1/16-1/23	1/24	1/25	1/26-1/27	1/28	1/29-2/1	2/2-2/3	2/4	
1 Ms. A	Gather Information	Forms Analysis; System Enhancements	Status Reports Due	First Draft Due	Edit First Draft	Second Draft Due	Edit Second Draft	Type Manual	Project Completed	
2 Mr. B		File Analysis; Memory Analysis								
3 Ms. C		Hardware Definition; Application								
4 Ms. D		Software Definition; Cost/Benefit Analysis								

8. Evaluation ✓

Establish a procedure or method of testing and evaluating the new system and a schedule for doing so. Anyone considering your proposal wants to know, How will I know if the system is working? How can I evaluate its performance?

EXAMPLES FOR SECTION 8: EVALUATION

Example 37

This acceptance test statement is crisp and informative.

ACCEPTANCE TEST

The Acceptance Test will be conducted according to the following criteria:

1. Conformance to report, file, and documentation designs that were approved by management prior to construction of system

84 PART TWO ANALYSIS

    2. Comparison of system output to a parallel run against the old manual system
        Discrepancies are expected to surface in parallel run due to changes in record-keeping methods and will be resolved by the analysis of selected records to determine proper cause

Example 38

If you had to schedule from this test plan for a non-preprinted call card analysis system what problems would you have?

SYSTEM TEST PLAN

Initial testing will utilize files of 100 or less records. Following maintenance and verification of accuracy, test file size will increase to that of production files. Maintenance and verification of accuracy by the senior systems consultant will signal the end of Phase I testing.

System testing will begin January 4, 1983, using test files created from the previous period's production files. Test reports will be sent to Marketing Data Services for final verification. Upon maintenance and final verification, final documentation and system turnover proceedings will be undertaken.

COMMENT

The writing is forthright, which is good. My questions are about time and schedules. The testing begins on January 4, but when does it end? There is no way to anticipate how long Phase I will be or how long it will take Marketing Data Services to give verification. The reader needs better information in order to schedule.

✔ 9. Alternatives

Structure a way to present a brief description of all other solutions considered. Include the major advantages and disadvantages of each. Format by list, chart, or pattern of organization so that the reader can compare the proposed solution with others considered.

EXAMPLES FOR SECTION 9: ALTERNATIVES

Example 39

Consider this first draft. Plan your own revisions and compare them with mine that follow in Example 40.

Alternatives:
1. <u>Contracting an outside vendor</u>. We could have a vendor microfiche all our necessary reports.

   Advantages:
   A. There would be no machinery to purchase or training of people.
   B. It would be cheaper than in-house production.

   Disadvantages:
   A. No profit would result from the contracting of other companies' microfiche jobs.
   B. Security of vital information would be threatened.
   C. There would be a time loss from transportation of jobs from company to microfiche shop.

   Summary: This would be a cheap way to microfiche but would not be good for self-sufficiency and profit.

2. <u>Purchasing extra printer</u>. This would keep the present system going; allowance would be made for the additional company by purchasing the extra printer.

   Advantages:
   A. There would be no risk of user non-acceptance.
   B. The printer would be cheaper than microfiche equipment.

   Disadvantages:
   A. There would be extra paperwork and the possibility of inflated paper costs.
   B. A storage building would have to be constructed for reports, but the stored reports could easily be damaged.
   C. The possible down time of a printer could result in excessive delay of reports to both companies up to 2 to 5 days.

   Summary: It would be cheap, but very inefficient.

86 PART TWO ANALYSIS

    3. <u>Do nothing.</u> Keep the present system as is.

       Advantages:
       A. There would be fewer costs and no extra risks.
       B. There would be no implementation tasks to carry out.

       Disadvantages:
       A. Turnaround time would have to be increased by at least 3 days for each report.
       B. A safe place for the storing of all reports would have to be found.

       Summary: This would not be beneficial for either company and would go against the company's goals.

Example 40

My objectives in editing this example are the following:

1. Adopt a more formal, business-like attitude in vocabulary and sentence structure
2. Correct the outlining so that it conforms to the standard format and way of numbering
3. Make the grammar and structure parallel
4. Tighten the writing and make it more direct
5. Use present tense.

Alternatives:

A. ~~1.~~ Contract~~ing~~ an outside vendor. ~~We could have~~ A vendor microfiches all our necessary reports.

    Advantages:

    1. ~~A.~~ ~~There would be no machinery to~~ Purchase of machinery and ~~or~~ training of people are not needed.

    2. ~~B.~~ Cost is less ~~It would be cheaper~~ than in-house production.

Disadvantages:

1. ~~X~~. No profit ~~would~~ result**s** from the contracting of other companies' microfiche jobs.

2. ~~X~~. Security of vital information ~~would be~~ **is** threatened.

3. ~~X~~. ~~There would be a~~ **T**ime **is** lost~~s~~ from transportation of jobs from company to microfiche shop.

Summary: (This would be) a (cheap way) to microfiche but would not be good for self-sufficiency and profit.
weak beginning — poor business language
Rewrite: While costing less, this alternative is not good for self-sufficiency and profit.

2. Purchasi~~ng~~**ed** extra printer. ~~This would keep~~ **T**he present system ~~going; allowance would be made for the additional company by purchasing the extra printer.~~ **continues to operate. The additional work caused by acquiring the new company is absorbed.**

Advantages:

1. ~~X~~. ~~There would be no~~ **The** risk of user non-acceptance **is avoided**.

2. ~~X~~. **A** ~~The~~ printer ~~would be cheaper~~ **costs less** than microfiche equipment.

Disadvantages:

1. ~~X~~. ~~There would be~~ **E**xtra paperwork **increases, and if** ~~and the possibility of inflated~~ paper costs ~~rise~~ **costs increase**.

2. ~~X~~. A storage building ~~would have~~ **needs** to be constructed for reports~~, but~~**. T**he stored reports ~~could~~ **can** easily be damaged.

3. ~~X~~. The possible down time of a printer ~~could~~ result**s** ~~in excessive~~ delay**s** **of up to 2 to 5 days for** reports to both companies. ~~up to 2 to 5 days.~~

Summary: It ~~would be cheap~~ **is less expensive**, but very inefficient.

3. <u>Do nothing.</u> Keep the present system as is.

Advantages:

1. Fewer costs and no risks are involved.
2. No implementation tasks are carried out.

Disadvantages:

1. Turnaround time increases by at least 3 days for each report.
2. A safer and larger place for storing of all reports must be found.

Summary: This alternative is beneficial for neither company and goes against each company's goals.

General Summary

Look anew at a proposal you have written or are going to write or review. Use you new awareness to structure the document, to improve your writing, and to be a good critic.

CHECKLIST: CHAPTER 5
The Proposal II

OUTLINE

1. PROBLEM STATEMENT AND ITS RELATION TO CURRENT OPERATIONS
   What is the problem?
   Why is it a problem?
   Why is the problem important?
   What is already known about the problem?
   Do not overstate.
   Avoid assumptions.
   Report correctly.

2. PROPOSED SOLUTION
   Fit solution to the problem
   Define scope of the solution.

3. OPERATIONAL REQUIREMENTS
   Describe procedures for manual and machine operations.
   Indicate work loads, personnel, procedures, and results.
   State the system's objectives.
   Clarify input and output required to meet the objectives.

4. OPERATING ENVIRONMENT
   Identify collection method.
   What hardware is required?
   How many of anything is needed?
   Where will items be placed?
   What software is required? Is it standard or must it be customized?

5. BENEFITS
   Show cost-savings and productivity benefits.

6. BUDGETS AND COSTS
   Be realistic.
   Think of every cost: people, equipment, space, training, development, etc.

7. IMPLEMENTATION PLAN
   Chart stages of design and implementation.

8. EVALUATION
   Establish a procedure of testing and evaluating and a schedule for doing so.

9. ALTERNATIVES
   Present all other solutions considered. Show major advantages and disadvantages of each.
   Format so the reader can compare the proposed solution with the alternatives.

6
Functional Specification I

What Is a Functional Specification and What Is Its Purpose?

A functional specification refines the ideas of a proposal into a detailed statement of particulars so that the client and system analyst can agree that the report accurately states what the client needs and wants and what the analyst intends to design and deliver. A functional specification serves as a contract between these two parties. Like any good contract, it protects both parties from entering into an agreement without a clear understanding of responsibilities and expectations.

In its final form, this document defines all major functions to be performed by the system. It describes how those functions relate to one another and to other components of the business involved; the system's input and output both in content and form; the scheduling, performance objectives, responsibilities, security, data retention, and communication network associated with the system.

A well-written functional specification is immensely helpful in designing and implementing a successful system. Even though those in data processing are eager to begin designing or programming and the client is eager to implement the system, now is the efficient time to set and revise specifications. It is easy and inexpensive to make changes at this time.

Like other documents in the computer system cycle, this report has several titles in addition to the one we are using; these include *external specifications, design specifications, requirement document, general design,* and *target document.* All "specify" the "functions" of the proposed system, and all record the agreement between the client and the system analyst.

Who Writes Functional Specifications and Who Reads Them?

The analyst actually writes and is responsible for producing the document, but the analyst and client should work together on its content. Both should read it and the document should represent both points of view. The analyst should not dictate to the client nor should the client arbitrarily specify to the analyst. Instead they should merge their knowledge to come to an understanding.

Anyone else who uses the system, manages it, or interfaces with it, should also read the document. Different people see different things; a user can spot a problem that a manager might miss and vice versa. By involving a complete or representative group of readers, you make future work easier. If everyone agrees now about the basic specifications of the system, you minimize future misunderstandings that cause delays or dissatisfaction.

Work Habits for Writing Good Functional Specifications

BE CURIOUS, PROBING, AND PATIENT

The client often has a great deal to learn about data processing in order to understand what the computer system can do and to judge the effectiveness of the proposed system. Likewise, the computer analyst must absorb and understand an enormous amount of unfamiliar information about the client's business in order to develop a system that serves the client better than the present way of doing business. For both to acquire this knowledge, each must be inquisitive, a good listener, and willing to spend time learning.

BE FLEXIBLE

Changes will occur up to the last minute—even while writing the last draft. Resist trying to stop everyone from having new thoughts, wanting alterations, or making deletions. Now is the proper time for invention. Encourage creativity and flexibility.

DO NOT ASSUME

Just because someone says a procedure is done a certain way for a certain reason does not mean you should not question it. In fact, if the information is being used for a specification, your job is to verify it. Do so by observing the procedure. Perform it if possible. Gather more than one person's explanation about it, and compare.

If someone makes a conclusion about an interface, or a point about security, or says something about responsibility, ask for the basis of the comment. Do you accept it? Good analysts are good thinkers. Do not be lazy or timid about inquiring into the what or why or how of things.

MAKE A SCHEDULE

Writing a functional specification can be a large task. Establish milestones so that you know where you are in the overall schedule. Milestones also let you feel rewarded when you complete a part of the whole.

KNOW YOUR AUDIENCE

How many different readers are you writing to? What interest does each have in reading a functional specification? Is one to use, manage, or own the system? The purpose of a functional specification is to have the readers agree. Write so that all can understand the report and act upon it.

You should also remember the range of readers while you investigate and learn the client's business. Certainly the user is the one to consult about a procedure that he or she performs, but the user may not be the person to consult about how a procedure interfaces with other departments or about system security. Your client expects you to be accurate; to be so, you must have accurate sources. Identify those sources; collect and interpret information—be an analyst, not a mere recorder.

Practice in Writing and Evaluating

ORGANIZE AND OUTLINE

No set-in-concrete formula exists for the content of a functional specification. Some people delay writing about certain topics until the design stage; others want to include such information in the functional specification. Our concern is not to debate where information should appear, but to evaluate how best to present information regardless of its position in the system documentation cycle.

For this purpose, we will consider a parts list of material common to a functional specification:

1. Identify the report and list its contents
2. Reintroduce the idea
3. Agree upon assumptions
4. Compile a glossary of technical terms
5. Picture input and output
6. Specify responsibilities
7. Identify hardware
8. Decide about data retention
9. Secure the system
10. Determine the system's audits

Whether your job is to write, review, or manage the writing of a functional specification, a definition of parts gives you a standard for content and form.

1. Identify the Report and List its Contents ✔

Your reader derives his or her first impression of your work from these two pieces. The title page should specifically state the project title and tell who you are. The table of contents should indicate the scope of the document and allow the reader easy access. Major sections should be titled and paged; subsections should be noted.

EXAMPLES FOR SECTION 1: IDENTIFY REPORT AND
LIST CONTENTS

Example 41

The following title page is not good enough. Jot down two reasons why I might say this.

```
              Voter Registration and
              Juror Selection System
                    X County


                    Bill Adams
                    Carol Brown
                    Jack Crow

                   July 23, 1982
```

COMMENT
1. The title is too general. It should say it is a specification document.
   Note: The actual report includes a juror payment program, yet this is omitted in the title. Any title should be accurate and complete.
2. The people listed have no titles. What positions do they hold? What company do they work for?
3. No table of contents is shown because none exists; the report just begins. As a result, the writers provide no way to reference the material.
4. The first impression this report gives is poor. The writers appear too informal and careless. I want to believe that the people working on analyzing and developing my system are precise and thorough. This beginning makes me wonder.

PART TWO ANALYSIS

Example 42

The following example makes a good first impression. If you agree, determine why it does.

DATA TECH CORPORATION

NON-PREPRINTED CALL CARD ANALYSIS SYSTEM

FUNCTIONAL SPECIFICATIONS

Computing Science 123
Software Engineering Project

University of Evansville
Evansville, Indiana

Submitted by John Smith
May 10, 1983

SPONSOR: Jack May

SPONSORING COMPANY: MAY COMPANY

COMMENT

Title Page: It is clear that this document is a functional specification. I know what company it refers to and who wrote it.

TABLE OF CONTENTS

	Page
INTRODUCTION	1
THE USER COMMUNITY	2
LOGICAL MODEL OF CURRENT SYSTEM	3
FUNCTIONAL DESCRIPTION	4
Figure 1 Overall Data Flow Diagram	5
Inputs	6
Outputs	12
Processing	12
Detailed Data Flow Diagrams	13
COST/BENEFIT ESTIMATES	16
IMPLEMENTATION PLAN	17
APPENDICES	19

COMMENT

Table of Contents: The page shows the scope of the document. The information is presented so that I can reference different parts of the document. The writer appears organized and careful; my first impression of it is good.

2. Reintroduce the Idea ✔

All kinds of things have happened since the original proposal was written and circulated. Other projects and ideas have been discussed, daily business has gone forward, memoranda and reports have been written, received, and read.

It is both a courtesy and a good business practice to begin by reminding the reader of the proposal. This briefing focuses the reader's attention and prepares him or her to understand your report.

A proper way to accomplish this review is to begin the functional specification with two sections from the proposal:

1. A statement of the problem and an explanation of its relation to current operations.
2. A statement of the proposed solution and its scope.

EXAMPLES FOR SECTION 2: REINTRODUCE THE IDEA

Example 43

The following example does a poor job of reintroducing the project. What problems do you see in this description? What suggestions would you make for revision?

General Description

The proposed student registration system will allow online registration of students into classes, keeping track of closed classes, and providing schedule information to counselors during that time. Provisions are made for performing online drops and adds up until the deadline date. A class roll may be produced at any time from the data. The final grades of each instructor will be read directly from grade sheets into the system from which grade reports and transcript stickers will be prepared.

COMMENT
1. The system will apparently provide three programs:
   a. student registration
   b. class roll
   c. grade reports and stickers

   It is not easy to see the three. The description needs to be formatted with a general statement about the "system" followed by a list of the three "programs."
2. The information mentioned under each program is inconsistent. For "online registration of students," the writer mentions the program's form—"online"—and tells something about what information will be included. But the comments about "a class roll" do not match. Is it also online? Is it soft copy? What information does it include?

3. What problems prompted this system? I have forgotten what the proposal said and do not want to look it up or see if I still have a copy. Tell me again about the current procedure, the problems with it, and how this system addresses those problems.
4. Language notes:
   a. The language is not precise. "System" should apply to the total concept and "programs" should apply to the three areas.
   b. The first and second sentences list information about the first program. Combine them and make the verb tenses alike. See rewrite.

REWRITE

Original Sentences 1 and 2

> The proposed student registration system will allow online registration of students into classes, keeping track of closed classes, and providing schedule information to counselors during that time. Provisions are made for performing online drops and adds up until the deadline date.

Rewrite of Sentences 1 and 2

The student registration system's set of programs has a program that will register students into classes, keep track of closed classes, provide counselors during registration with schedule information, and make drops and adds of classes.

COMMENT ON REWRITE

The verbs "register," "keep," "provide," and "drop" are now in the same tense and form. In the original, the verbs tenses are mixed: "will allow" then "keeping" then "providing" then "are made."

In the original, the writer also mixes voice; the first sentence is active voice ("system will allow"); the second sentence is passive voice ("Provisions are made"). Whenever possible, write in active voice.

Example 44

A very effective way to brief the reader is to repeat, without apology or without change, the same material that began the proposal. For example, the writer of the proposal Preludes to Weaving (see p. 65) does this. Her functional specification begins (after a title page and table of contents) as follows:

> PROBLEM DEFINITION
>
> Each time a weaver envisions a pattern for a piece of cloth, the actual weaving must be delayed until the weaver completes preliminary tasks. Problems exist . . .
>
> RELATIONSHIP OF PROBLEMS TO CURRENT OPERATIONS
>
> A weaver uses graph paper and colored pencils to draw a pattern draft:
>   1. Mental adjustments must be made . . .
>
> PROPOSED SOLUTION TO THE PROBLEM
>
> The proposed system, Preludes to Weaving, demonstrates the following characteristics . . .

COMMENT
The format and clear writing make the reader once again alert to the project and prepared to read this specification report.

3. Agree upon Assumptions

What seems likely, practical, sensible, or inexpensive to one person may not appear that way to another. Therefore, the client and analyst need to record what they both assume about this proposed system:

> What will the system cost?
> How many people will be needed to operate the system?
> How much and what kind of hardware will the system need to operate?
> How long will it take to design and implement the system?
> How much training is necessary to have company people use the system?
> Where and how can people, terminals, and storage be placed?

Basic questions like these need to be asked and answered in order for system analysis to go forward and be based on a real understanding between client and analyst. The risk of assuming can be the development of an unsuitable and ineffective system.

EXAMPLES FOR SECTION 3: AGREE UPON ASSUMPTIONS

Example 45

The following is a good example of recording assumptions. The project is a CAI program for solving linear programming problems using the graphical method. Determine what specifications are tied down and why this understanding is essential.

```
                    SECTION III
                  SYSTEM FUNCTIONS
General Assumptions
     Project Users:
          1. Student users have been introduced to the graphi-
             cal method of solving LP problems through clas-
             sroom lecture.
          2. Student users have at least a general knowledge of
             college-level algebra.
          3. Student users have been instructed on the use of the
             Apple II Plus computer and are familiar with the
             procedures for running programs on diskette.
          4. The student's LP problem will consist of:
             *Objective function with a maximum of two vari-
             ables.
             *Problem constraints up to a maximum of five.
     Project Leader:
          5. Dr. Stuart will make the arrangements for the stu-
             dents' program and computer use.
     Project Designer:
          1. The designer will solve the problem by having the
             computer use the Simplex method. The results will
             verify the solutions arrived at by students' using
             the graphical method.
          2. The designer will use the programming language Ap-
             plesoft BASIC and the high-resolution graphics
             capabilities.
```

COMMENT
The writing and the format are clear. The analyst obviously has discussed the basic qualifications of the proposed system with the client. These understandings allow the system to be tailored to the user's needs. The analyst gains assurance that the system he or she develops will satisfy the client.

4. Compile a Glossary of Technical Terms ✓

Two groups read a functional specification: one group (the client) may not know anything about computers; the other group (data processors) are computer experts. Your goal is to write so both groups understand. Your problem is that you must write about computers, so you must use some technical language. One way to allow all readers to follow the discussion is to place a glossary in the report, near the beginning or at the end. If you choose the end of the report, remember to list it in the table of contents so the reader will know it is available. Never assume that the reader will look ahead or seek out any information.

EXAMPLES FOR SECTION 4: GLOSSARY OF TECHNICAL TERMS

Example 46

The intention of this glossary is good. It means to define terms common and necessary for a discussion of a computer system. The problem is that it does not accomplish its intention. What problems do you see?

```
GLOSSARY
crt—cathode ray tube; same as a television screen
terminal—a crt with a typewriter keyboard connected to it
disk—a magnetic data storage device
online—files are updated at the time of input rather than having
       transactions collected and updated all at once at the
       end of the day (batch processing)
```

COMMENT
1. If such elementary terms as "crt" and "disk" must be defined, we can assume that the client/reader has no familiarity with computers. Given this audience, the definitions are not effective. For example, the "online" definition talks about "input" and "batch processing" and "files." The reader will not understand these technical terms; consequently he or she will not understand the definition.
2. Three oversights make the writer appear careless: 1. the glossary is not alphabetized; 2. the format does not align items; 3. the format does not distinguish the term from the definition. (Capitalization separates the two in the revision.) Think how a page will appear to the reader. What impression will it make? Visualizing will cause you to present information more effectively.
3. Be consistent. The last entry in this glossary is a sentence. The others are parts of sentences. Either is all right; just be regular.
4. When formatting, plan for margins. In this glossary, the margins are ragged. Determine the longest word, then line up the definitions based on that spacing. For example, look at the "crt" and "terminal" definitions. The spacing looks like an amateur did it. You do not want your client to think an amateur is doing the analysis. (Compare the example with the rewrite.)
5. Care about appearances. The page is an image of the way you think. Appear organized and logical.

REWRITE

CRT   Acronym for Cathode Ray Tube; a television screen commonly used with a keyboard to display information (data) typed into the computer; part of a "terminal"

MAGNETIC DISK   A plastic or metal surface coated with a magnetic compound; data (information) recorded by magnetized dot patterns, remains stored on disk; can be reread, revised, or deleted

PART TWO   ANALYSIS

CHECKLIST: CHAPTER 6
Functional Specification I

DEFINITION AND FUNCTION	Refines proposal into a detailed statement of particulars. Enables client and analyst to agree about needs and design of proposed system.
WRITER	System analyst. But analyst and client should work together on content.
AUDIENCE	Client. Anyone else who uses, manages, or interfaces with the system.
GOOD WORK HABITS	Be curious, probing, and patient. Be flexible. Do not assume. Make a schedule. Know your audience.
OUTLINE	
1. IDENTIFY REPORT AND LIST CONTENTS	Provide a title page and state the title. Identify the author(s). Provide a table of contents, indicate the document's scope. Allow easy access. Provide a title for major sections. Note subsections.
2. REINTRODUCE IDEA	Remind reader of the proposal. Review problem statement and how the problem relates to current operations, and proposed solution.
3. AGREE UPON ASSUMPTIONS	Record both client's and analyst's assumptions about proposed system: cost, people, training, hardware, software, place, schedules, etc.
4. CONSTRUCT A GLOSSARY FOR TECHNICAL TERMS	Provide definitions for nontechnical readers. Alphabetize. Format: anticipate margins; make easy to read. Be consistent in form of definition: all sentences or all phrases, etc.

7
Functional Specification II

5. Picture Input and Output ✓

To the analyst, talking about input/output may seem like beginning at the end, but to the client, it is beginning with what is most important: the data the system will require and provide. If you can satisfy that curiosity and gain the client's approval, you will clear the way to have the client's attention for other matters.

Picture the input and output. Show size, format, and information. Once you give the client concrete examples to review, you both can communicate specifically and reach agreement.

```
EXAMPLES FOR SECTION 5: PICTURE INPUT AND
OUTPUT
```

```
Example 47
```

The following example illustrates the need to picture information. I cannot begin to imagine this report, much less decide if this form is better than the way I presently do business. My problems as a reader are stated in the text.

```
Patient Summary Report (PSR)

   The patient summary report is the cumulative report of all of
a patient's verified tests; it is to be inserted in the pa-
tient's chart.
```

COMMENT
What does it look like? How big is it? What does "inserted" mean? Is it to fit into the patient's chart in some way?

The patient's name, identification number, sex, age, location, admitting doctor, and admitting diagnosis appear at the top of each page, along with the date and time the report is printed.

COMMENT
How do all these items "appear at the top of each page"? Does that mean each page of every new report or each page of the same report?

The report shows the test reporting name, result name, result units, normal ranges, specimen type, collection data and time for those results which the methodology file states are to be reported on the PSR.

COMMENT
How does the report "show" the test reporting name, etc.? Is it checked, circled, or written in? I do not understand the last half of this sentence. Does it say the methodology file states when the "time" is to be reported, or does it mean that the methodology file states that all this information must be on this report?

Abnormal results will be flagged with any character, e.g., H (high) and L (low).

COMMENT
What does "flagged" mean? In some different color? With a capital letter? How can something be flagged "with any character"? Does that mean that I can choose any character I want? If so, how does anyone else know what my "character" means?

The number of days to be included in a permanent report is defined by the doctor. If a patient has no tests on a given day, that day is not counted and does not appear on the report.

COMMENT
I do not understand. What does the doctor's definition have to do with missed days? How do you know a day was missed if it does not "appear"?

SUMMARY COMMENT
The only way I can begin to evaluate this report is to get out a piece of paper and map out the information according to what directions are given. But I do not want to do this, and I should not have to. Besides, having no idea how the information is to be placed, I will only be guessing. My correct action is to return this report to the system analyst and ask that the information be presented in a form that I can evaluate.

Example 48

The following example illustrates the value of using pictures. The replicas allow the information to be checked and the format considered. In this case, the pictures are not well thought out, but having them allows the client and analyst to talk about change. My comments appear after each illustration. These specifications are for a company payroll program.

DESCRIPTION OF OUTPUT

Paychecks: The paychecks will be standard checks in this form:

```
+-----------------------------------------------------------+
|                                                           |
|                                          Check No. ____   |
|                                                           |
|   Pay to the order of _____   $ _____    |
|                                                           |
|                                                           |
|                       Signed: _____     |
|                                                           |
+-----------------------------------------------------------+
```

COMMENT
Does "standard checks" mean standard for this company or standard by some other measure? No company name appears on this mock-up. Who is responsible for payment? This example must be more accurate. Why not photocopy the checks if they are standard company checks?

Deduction Statement: The deduction statement will accompany the paycheck and list the deductions for the current pay period and the cumulative deductions to date.

```
+-----------------------------------------------------------+
|                                                           |
|                     Deduction Statement                   |
|                                                           |
|      Smith, Joe, B.          Pay Period No. _____    |
|                                                           |
|          This period                   Total to date      |
|                                                           |
|      Social Security  $ _____          $ _____            |
|      State Taxes      $ _____          $ _____            |
|      Federal Taxes    $ _____          $ _____            |
|                                                           |
+-----------------------------------------------------------+
```

COMMENT

The title needs to be more accurate (Employee Deduction Statement?) to match the more specific example that follows, "Department Totals Sheet."

The introduction to this deduction statement says this statement "will accompany the paycheck." What does that mean? Will it be attached? Will it be included in the envelope? Restructure and rework this form:

1. Format so items line up.
2. Add information that appears necessary as you read the next two forms (for example, include department number, make a better title, and add totals).
3. Formalize the document by punctuating, capitalizing, and underlining.

Rewrite

```
                    Employee Deduction Statement


    Employee: Smith, Joe, B.
    Department No. _____              Pay Period: _____


    Deductions:      Pay Period: _____   Annual Total to Date:

    Soc. Sec.  $ _____  _____          $ _____
    St. Tax.   $ _____  _____          $ _____
    Fed. Tax   $ _____  _____          $ _____

    Total:                                         Total: _____
```

Department Totals: The Department Totals Sheet presents the totals of all deductions and payments made to the employees of that department.

```
┌─────────────────────────────────────────────────────────┐
│              Department Totals Sheet                    │
│                                                         │
│   Dept. No. _____ TOTALS                              │
│                                                         │
│   Employee No.      Deductions      Payment             │
│                                                         │
│    This period      To date      This period   To date  │
│                                                         │
│     Soc. Sec. $_____    $_____                        │
│     St. Tax   $_____    $_____                        │
│     Fed. Tax  $_____    $_____                        │
│                                                         │
│                                     $_____    $_____  │
└─────────────────────────────────────────────────────────┘
```

COMMENT

Make the title specific, but herein lies a problem. What do "Deductions" and "Payment" mean? Obviously, "deductions" mean Social Security, State Tax, and Federal Tax, but does "Payment" mean of these three taxes or does it mean the "pay" of the employee? Make the form clear so one can evaluate it.

Use spacing and format to present information clearly:

1. Align the items.
2. Add a line to show the department total for this pay period and for the year to date.
3. Make all the forms consistent. For example, the original "Deduction Statement" form writes out "State Taxes"; this form writes "St. Tax."

Company Totals: (The information continues in the same way and has the same problems.)

SUMMARY COMMENT

This example illustrates how pictures help people communicate. Even though I have questions and criticisms of the information, the method is good because I can use the form to comment, disagree, and make changes. It is an effective working copy.

PART TWO ANALYSIS

Example 49

The following is a statement of output from a functional specification for a student registration system. Imagine you are the client reading this. How well can you "picture" the report? What questions do you have about format, using the form, etc.?

Student Grade Report: The student grade report will be prepared from the machine-readable grade sheets filled in by the instructors and from other student information. A student grade report is sent to each student following the close of the semester to inform him or her of the grades. It is a four-part carbonless form, with the original going to the student, one copy to the counselor, and two copies to the dean. The fields are:

1. Student number
2. Student name
3. Address 1
4. Address 2
5. City
6. State
7. Zip code
8. Course number
9. Department name
10. Course title
11. Credit hours
12. Grade
13. Honor points
14. Total hours attempted
15. Total hours passed
16. Total honor points
17. Total hours producing honor points
18. Semester hours attempted
19. Semester hours passed
20. Semester honor points
21. Semester hours producing honor points

COMMENT

Appearances are sometimes deceiving. At first glance, this statement looks good—lots of white space and easy to read. But in reality, I cannot picture the report. What is its size, shape, layout? If I could see how the "fields" are placed on the page, I could then begin to evaluate the report.

My most important question is about the "machine-readable grade sheets" mentioned in the opening statement. (Nowhere in this functional specification did an example of the "sheets" appear.) What are these sheets? How does the instructor "fill in" the grades? Who fills in the information "from other student information"?

Example 50

The following example shows an effective use of input/output illustrations. These printed versions of what will appear on the CRT screen are for a CAI system for solving linear programming problems using the graphical method. How is the example useful to a client?

```
              SOLVING
     LINEAR PROGRAMMING PROBLEMS
               USING
        THE GRAPHICAL METHOD
```

THIS PROGRAM IS DESIGNED TO GIVE YOU PRACTICE IN SOLVING LINEAR PROGRAMMING PROBLEMS USING THE GRAPHICAL METHOD.

FOR THIS PROGRAM TO BE HELPFUL, YOU NEED TO HAVE THE FOLLOWING:

1. A BASIC KNOWLEDGE OF HOW TO SOLVE LP PROBLEMS USING THE GRAPHICAL METHOD

2. A PREVIOUSLY FORMATTED LP PROBLEM WITH 2 VARIABLES AND NO MORE THAN 5 CONSTRAINTS

3. A PENCIL AND PAPER FOR MAKING YOUR CALCULATIONS

PRESS 'RETURN' TO CONTINUE.

THE STEPS FOR SOLVING LP PROBLEMS GRAPHICALLY ARE AS FOLLOWS:

1. PLOT THE CONSTRAINTS FIRST AS EQUALITIES, THEN AS INEQUALITIES.

2. IDENTIFY THE FEASIBLE REGION AND THE EXTREME POINTS.

3. PLOT OBJECTIVE FUNCTION ALTERNATIVES.

4. IDENTIFY THE OPTIMAL EXTREME POINT(S).

5. SOLVE FOR THE EXTREME POINT COORDINATES.

6. SUBSTITUTE THESE COORDINATES, THE VALUES OF THE TWO VARIABLES, INTO THE OBJECTIVE FUNCTION TO DETERMINE ITS OPTIMAL VALUE.

PRESS 'RETURN' TO CONTINUE.

PERIODICALLY YOU WILL BE ASKED TO INDICATE WHETHER YOU WISH
TO CONTINUE WITH THE PROGRAM BY ENTERING 'Y' OR 'N'.

AN 'N' ENTRY WILL TERMINATE THE PROGRAM IMMEDIATELY.

DO YOU WISH TO CONTINUE (Y OR N)?

THIS PROGRAM ARBITRARILY ASSIGNS THE NAME 'X1' TO THE FIRST
VARIABLE AND 'X2' TO THE SECOND VARIABLE.

YOUR FIRST TASK IS TO ENTER THE OBJECTIVE FUNCTION OF YOUR
LP PROBLEM.

PRESS 'RETURN' TO CONTINUE.

AN EXAMPLE OF HOW TO ENTER THE OBJECTIVE FUNCTION FOLLOWS:

EXAMPLE: MAXIMIZE 2000X1 + 500X2

WHAT IS THE X1 COEFFICIENT? 200

WHAT IS THE X2 COEFFICIENT? 500

THE OBJECTIVE FUNCTION ENTERED IS MAXIMIZE 200X1 + 500X2

IS THIS CORRECT (Y OR N)? Y

PRESS 'RETURN' TO CONTINUE.

COMMENT
The analyst gives the client a clear picture of what the input/output screen will look like. Hence, the client can determine if the material is accurate and usable. If changes must be made, the printed versions of the screens are easy to use.

6. Specify Responsibilities

The client, user, or manager must foresee what the new system means in terms of people, scheduling, and expense. Is there enough time to process certain data before it is due somewhere else? Can the person or department accomplish a task by the time designated? Can the people specified for certain tasks manage the new work in addition to the work they are now doing? Does the budget allow new people to be hired where necessary? Is money available for training?

The challenge is to write so that managers and users understand their responsibilities to the system once it is up and running.

You may organize the responsibilities by departments, by individuals, or by tracing input and output. No single way is best for everything. Adjust your presentation to suit the audience and the information.

EXAMPLES FOR SECTION 6: SPECIFY RESPONSIBILITIES

Example 51

In this example, the decision to use a table is a good one; however, the execution of the table is not effective. Decide what is useful and what is unclear or not said.

RESPONSIBILITIES

In order to maintain accurate, up-to-the-minute information in the files to be used in creating the reports, employees in the various user departments must enter the necessary additions, deletions, and revisions to the computer as soon as possible. The following table contains a description of the information to be entered from each department, the purpose of the information, the reports and/or document that will be generated, and how often and in what form these reports will be produced.

DATA ENTERED/ USER DEPT.	PURPOSE OF INFORMATION	REPORT OR DOCUMENT
Reorders– purchasing	Update quantity level on inventory	Inventory status/ exception report Daily

(The report continues in this way.)

COMMENT

A writer must write what he or she promises. The introduction to the chart says the "following table" will "describe" five things:

1. Information entered and department making entry
2. Purpose of information
3. Reports generated
4. How often reports generated
5. Form reports take

The chart does not give this information.

1. This material (item 1) is not clearly presented. I assume that "information" is the same as "data entered" in column one, but the "information" is not distinguished from the user "department."
2. I do not find the "purpose of information" (item 2) anywhere.
3. I cannot identify the "reports" in column three.
4,5. These items appear nowhere.

A rewrite follows that suggests a way to improve this example as well as to make the introduction less wordy.

Rewrite

RESPONSIBILITIES

Inventory:
To maintain accurate file information and create accurate reports, employees in various user departments must enter into the computer at designated times additions, deletions, and revisions to inventory. The following table identifies responsibilities for both input and output.

		INPUT		
Data Entered	Dept./Person Responsible	Form	When	Where Available/Delivered
Reorders	Purchasing/ Clerk	On-line	10:00 A.M. 3:00 P.M. daily	———

		OUTPUT		
Data	Dept./Person Responsible	Form	When	Where Available/Delivered
———	———	———	———	———

COMMENT
The rewrite separates input from output in order to clarify information and give equal information about both.

It corrects the flaws of the original table: mixing input and output, failing to say "how often" and "in what form" the input and output appear and failing to identify who is responsible for output.

The opening comment is reduced.

Example 52

Declaring responsibilities is good, but this writer needs to go into more detail and be more specific. See comments.

RESPONSIBILITIES

Inventory Management:
At the conclusion of each working day, an employee in the Purchasing Department will give Data Entry a record of all additions, deletions, and modifications to inventory.

COMMENT
Be specific about time. Does "conclusion of . . . day" mean 4:30 P.M., closing time, or what? Which "employee" will give a "record"? How is that employee designated? How does the employee know he or she is supposed to do this task? What does "give" mean? Does the employee call in or carry a report to the Data Entry Department?

Data Entry will then process all of these transactions.

COMMENT
Does "then": mean immediately? If not, when will the transactions be processed?

After Data Entry has completed these transactions and notified the Computer Center of the completed task, two printouts of the "Out-of-Stock/Below Minimum Report" will be run and delivered to the Purchasing and Customer Service Departments by an employee in the Computer Center.

COMMENT
What is the connection between Data Entry completing the task and notifying the Computer Center? Is the Data Entry Department or the Computer Center responsible for "running" the report? Are two printouts delivered to one department (the Purchasing and Customer Service Department) or is one printout delivered to the Purchasing Department and one printout delivered to Customer Service? Who specifically delivers the report?

SUMMARY COMMENT
I have no quarrel with the writer's decision to employ a narrative (use a paragraph form), but I do expect the writer to be more precise and accurate.

In the rewrite I format information so it is easier to see. My design separates and highlights information. I make up facts in order to be specific.

Rewrite

RESPONSIBILITIES

Inventory Management:

Input:
By 4:30 P.M. of each working day, the manager of the Purchasing Department will send to the Data Entry Department the pink carbon copy of the inventory sheet (see Appendix 1C). This sheet shows the Department's additions, deletions, and modifications to inventory from 4:00 P.M. the previous work day to 4:00 P.M. this work day.

Output:
Each working day the Data Entry Department will process the information on the inventory sheet and produce by 9:30 A.M. two printouts:
 1. Out-of-Stock Report
 2. Below-Minimum Report
    (See Appendices 2C and 3C)

The Data Entry Department will deliver by 10:00 A.M. of each working day one copy of the Out-of-Stock Report to the Customer Service Department. The Purchasing Department will receive by the same time one copy of each of the two reports.

SUMMARY COMMENT
I keep the narrative form, but specify the material and divide input and output. The appendices (not shown) will show mock-ups of new forms and/or samples of presently used forms. Consequently, the client has something concrete to evaluate.

Example 53

The following example is impossible to read. The single spacing with nothing highlighted or separated makes the text so dense that I am reluctant to wade through it. Once I do start, the explanation of the "process" is unclear and confusing. Two alternatives for revision follow the example.

```
                         PROCESSING
The admissions office personnel will enter the student file as
the student makes application to the college. This file may be
updated at any time by persons with the proper security. The
student's information must be entered before enrollment be-
gins. The registrar will update the class schedule before the
enrollment date. The class maximum will be entered at this time,
but may be changed at any time. This update must be done before a
class schedule can be printed. After the update, hard-copy
class schedules will be produced for distribution. At enroll-
ment time, the counselors will enroll the students at a termi-
nal. The counselor will have access to his counselee's file and
to the current class schedule on the computer. After registra-
tion, the class lists will be produced for distribution the next
morning. The class lists will also be produced at the end of the
drop period and the end of the add period. They may be produced at
other times on demand. At the middle and at the end of the semes-
ter, grade sheets on machine-readable forms will be given to all
instructors. The instructors will mark the grade sheets and
return them for processing. When all grade sheets are returned,
the midsemester or final student grade reports will be pro-
duced. At the end of the semester, the transcript stickers are
produced and delivered to the Dean's office to be affixed to the
transcript. At all points of input and output, appropriate data
editing will occur. Admissions office personnel, registrar's
office personnel, and faculty will be trained in the use of the
CRT terminal in this system—both in terms of input and out-
put.
```

REWRITE
I use a classification and division pattern to separate the processes from one another and divide each process. The client/user/manager can see what the new system will mean in terms of people and workloads. Thus he or she can locate problems. Two ways of classifying are used:
1. Who does the process?
2. When is the process done?

A writer can decide which to use by determining what the reader most needs to understand.

Rewrite 1 Who does the process?

STUDENT REGISTRATION SYSTEM
Processing Responsibilities

I. Admissions Office
   A. Input
      1. File Name: Student File
         a. When entered:
            Prior to each registration
         b. Form:
            Online
         c. When updated:
            Week 3 of each semester
         d. Who enters and updates:
            Office personnel
      2. (Same format continues)
   B. Output
      1. File Name: Student File
         a. Who orders file:
            Admissions office
         b. Available when
            Week 4 of each semester
         c. Form:
            Print out
         d. Who receives file:
            Student and student's counselor
         e. Who distributes file:
            Admissions office by campus mail
         f. Who responsible for data:
            Admissions office
II. Registrar's Office
    (Same format)
III. Instructors
     (Same format)

Rewrite 2 When is the process done?

PART TWO ANALYSIS

STUDENT REGISTRATION SYSTEM

Processing Responsibilities

I. Prior to Each Semester Registration
   A. Admissions Office
      1. Input
         a. File name: Student file
         b. Input form: Online
         c. When input: Week 3 of each semester
         d. Who input and updates: Admissions office
         e. When updated: Last week of each semester
      2. Output
         a. File name: Student file
         b. When available: Week 4 of each semester
         c. Who orders file: Admissions office
         d. File form: Print out
         e. How file distributed: Campus mail
         f. Who distributes file: Admissions office
         g. When file distributed: Week 4 of each semester
         h. Who receives file: Student and student's counselor
         i. Who responsible for data: Admissions office
   B. Registrar's Office
      1. Input
         a.
         b.
      2. Output
         a.
         b.
   C. Instructors
      1. Input
         a.
         b.
      2. Output
         a.
         b.
II. During Registration
    (Same format)
III. During Each Semester
     (Same format)
IV. End of Each Semester
    (Same format)

✔ 7. Identify Hardware

The client/user must know what hardware is needed, where it needs to be placed, and what environment it needs to operate efficiently.

EXAMPLES FOR SECTION 7: IDENTIFY HARDWARE

Example 54

How do you judge this example from an integrated information system of customer accounts?

> Hardware:
> Your existing IBM 4331 will be utilized for the new information system. Six new CRT terminals (IBM 3278) will be purchased; one each will be placed in the following departments: Marketing, DDA, Savings, Cashiers, Accounting, Loans. Desk space will be needed for each terminal, to be connected directly to the IBM 4331.

COMMENT
The information is straightforward and clear. As a result, the client knows to plan for buying and to plan for space.

Example 55

How useful is this statement to you as a client or user or manager?

> HARDWARE SELECTION
> Since the client's company presently has no automated system, the company will acquire a system similar to the one used to develop the client's system, an Apple II Plus. The extensive files required for the system dictate the selection of a hard disk system of at least 5 mg.
>
> For the target implementation system, the Apple III model is recommended because its operating system interfaces easily with the hard disk system. Other advantages of the Apple III are its 128K standard RAM and the availability of hardware support for the Apple in St. Petersburg, Florida, where the system is being implemented.

COMMENT
It is good that the writer gives the reasons for choosing the particular system. However, the report does not mention where the system needs to be placed and what environment it requires. If space and environment are not problems,

say so. The client or manager then knows this or is reminded that such matters have been discussed and agreed upon.

Example 56

Comments follow this example from an information retrieval project.

HARDWARE

To accomplish this change, the current information which is stored on a magnetic tape will be transferred to an ABC model 5100 high speed disk to be accessed by an ABC 2150 equipped with ABC 3680, 3685, 3900, and 4020 peripherals and having multi-processing VX/T41 processing capabilities. The user terminals will be ABC 7983 VDU terminals located at each ABC branch office and connected via ARR long distance lines. Each branch office will have an ABC 1896B printer to make hard-copy information. On-the-road sales personnel will be equipped with portable printing terminals with built-in acoustic couplers for access to the data base via modems.

COMMENT

Does the reader understand the technical terms "modems," "VDU terminals," "high speed disk," "multi-processing VX/T41 processing capabilities," etc.? If not, this section does not inform the reader.

8. Decide about Data Retention

The user must understand how the data will be stored, what form the stored data will be in, and what back up exists for the stored data.

Assume the user is to have an online system:

How long will the data remain online?
How is the data removed from online—automatically or manually? When is the data removed?
What data is stored offline? What form is it in? How often is it entered into storage? How long will it be stored? Who monitors the storage process?
What environment is needed for offline or off-site storage?

EXAMPLES FOR SECTION 8: DECIDE ABOUT DATA RETENTION

Example 57

For a small or individual system, the statement can be simple. Consider this explanation for the system, "Preludes To Weaving."

Data Retention

The user will determine what data will be kept on his or her diskette and for what length of time. These same provisions will apply to the duplicate copy of the diskette.

COMMENT
While the explanation is basically adequate, the user may wonder what is a "duplicate copy." How does one make a "duplicate"? How often must one duplicate the "data"?

Example 58

This example is basically effective. Why do I say this? What could be improved?

Data Retention

The data stored by the bank will be maintained on disk storage. However, the disk storage will be backed up by both a paper copy and a tape copy.

For easy access, the disks are stored in the Data Processing Department. The paper copy is kept at a security building near the bank. The tapes are stored in the fireproof vault at the bank.

All data pertaining to current customers will be stored on disk as well as on paper and tape. Current customer data will constantly be available on disk storage. However, once a customer terminates his or her affiliation with the bank, his or her data are removed from disk storage.

9. Secure the System ✔

Your responsibility is to make clear what security means in terms of procedure and expense:

> How does one gain access to the terminal? Is it by key, card, or cipher locks?
> How are the terminals secured? Do they sit in open space—in rooms by themselves? Can the space be secured when the business is closed?
> How are materials and supplies secured?

PART TWO ANALYSIS

How is the network secured? Can anyone obtain access to all information in the system or is a user limited only to certain information? If the latter is true, is a password used to gain limited access? If not, what is used?

These and other appropriate questions force the client to anticipate space, personnel, and budget needs. In addition, they help the client realize what changes or precautions must be planned.

EXAMPLES FOR SECTION 9: SECURE THE SYSTEM

Example 59

How much do you know from this statement? Do you judge it effective? If so, why? If not, why?

SECURITY

<u>Mainframe Security</u>:
The security for the main computer will remain the same as it has been in the past.

<u>Terminal Security</u>:
One terminal each will be placed in the following areas, and the named personnel will be responsible for its security by a key-locking device.

President's Office	Ms. A
Marketing Office	Ms. B
Operations Department	Mr. C
Data Processing Department	Mr. D
Lending Office	Mr. E
Teller Area	Ms. F

These persons have the responsibility of unlocking the terminals for use each morning when the bank opens and of relocking the terminals once the bank closes. Access to the terminals is available to all bank personnel during normal banking hours.

<u>Information Security</u>:
As information is now readily available via the CRT terminals, extra security is necessary to protect customer confidentiality. Two measures will protect this information.

1. To obtain customer information from a terminal, a password must first be typed to show authorization. The pass-

7 FUNCTIONAL SPECIFICATION II   123

    word will change monthly and will be known only to bank personnel.
2. To use the terminals after banking hours, permission must be obtained from the Controller of Data Processing, Mr. A.

COMMENT

Dividing the types of security into "mainframe," "terminal," and "information" is effective. The information is concrete; the reader knows what to expect and can plan.

Example 60

This example charts information. It is easy to read, easy to understand, and most effective.

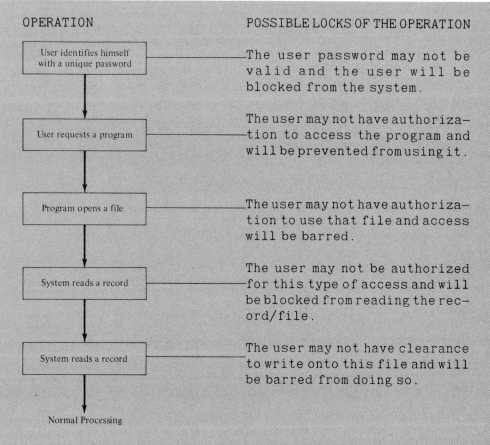

Figure 1   System of Internal Locks

PROGRAMMED LOCKS

1. User Identification.
   For anyone to use the computer system, he must first identify himself to the computer through use of a password. The identification process is shown in Figure 2.

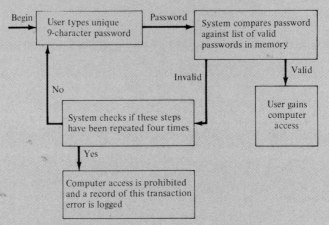

Figure 2   Identification Process

✔ 10. Determine the System's Audits

Cover all information necessary for the client to be assured that the system will be satisfactorily inspected and verified. How will this process occur? What data audits will be run? Will they be run manually or automatically?

A functional specification must be written to several audiences. The hands-on user may not care about audits, but managers and people in the legal department certainly do.

EXAMPLES FOR SECTION 10: DETERMINE THE
SYSTEM'S AUDITS

Example 61

This example is not effective because it is not specific. Imagine yourself the client. What do you not understand? What questions do you have?

AUDITS

1. A list of the daily transactions on the voter registration file
2. A report showing the starting point of selections in the eligible juror pool and adherence to the algorithm

3. A check (by the clerk of the court) of the list of selected jurors, time of service, jury served on, and the amount of reimbursements
4. Maintenance of a juror check register (by the auditor)
5. Other audits in accordance with current practices

General Summary

Look again at a functional specification you have written or one you are writing, managing, or producing. How good is it as a contract? Will both you and the client be well served? Have you included the proper and necessary information and formatted so that it is easy to use and read?

PART TWO ANALYSIS

CHECKLIST: CHAPTER 7
Functional Specification II

OUTLINE

5. PICTURE INPUT AND OUTPUT

   Show size, format, and information.

6. SPECIFY RESPONSIBILITIES

   Let client, user, or manager understand what the new system means in terms of people, scheduling, and expense.

   Organize responsibilities to suit audience and information: by departments, by individuals, by tracing input and output, etc.

7. IDENTIFY HARDWARE

   Specify hardware: its location and environment.

8. DECIDE ABOUT DATA RETENTION

   Tell how data will be stored: the form and backup.
   Who monitors storage process?
   How often are data entered into storage?
   How long are data stored?
   What environment does stored data need?

9. SECURE THE SYSTEM

   What does security mean in terms of procedure and expense?
   How are terminals, materials, networks, etc., secured?

10. DETERMINE THE SYSTEM'S AUDITS

    Assure the client that the system will be inspected and verified.
    Determine how this process will be done.

PART THREE

DESIGN

A client and analyst can talk till the cows come home about input and output, where to place the terminals, how to retain data, and how to secure a system—but these discussions do not cause a system to be implemented. Designs do.

The design permits the system to progress from being something talked about into something that exists. It is no wonder that good designers enjoy prestige and respect; they are the artists of the computer world. They give form to abstract ideas.

The task can be enormous. The designer studies the functional specification to understand the constraints set by time, space, budget, or management. He or she assimilates this information to design a system that solves the problem, is practical, and is efficient. If the system is a sizable one, you can recognize the complexity of the task and the talent required to perform the task well.

For a system to have longevity, it needs a good design and good design documentation. During its lifetime, the system will be repaired, modified, even redesigned, and maybe imitated. Good design documentation thereby extends the system's life. Without it, the system remains opaque, mysterious, noncommunicative, and will finally be abandoned because no one can communicate with or about it. The people who designed the system have moved on to other projects or have forgotten how it was created. It is expensive and wasteful to create systems that do not have long life.

Design traditionally is divided into two phases. A formal document is written to record the work of each phase:

WORK PHASE	DOCUMENT
System design	System specification
Program design	Program specification

In reality, system and program design often overlap. Nevertheless they are two separate activities. They are sequential; each has its function, audience, and specific content.

We shall study the system specification because its content is broader, but a stage of program design will also be included in our discussion. In the design stage two levels of program specification exist. One appears in the system specification, covering the interrelations of programs. It tells how programs feed each other and explains what the programs are for. The second makes up the program specification and states what a program does within itself.

8
System Specification I

What Is a System Specification and What Is Its Function?

A system specification is the system's major technical document. It is the reference for building all programs, the source for the operations manual, and the origin of future system modification.

Good documentation serves as history for the system. It describes the system's origins. During the system's life cycle, an analyst, manufacturer, or designer may want to study a particular part of the system, or learn how several parts are interdependent, or understand why one design was chosen rather than some other. A good system specification answers such questions. It makes the system's use independent of its original designers.

System specification assists in duplication. Someone may wish to incorporate a component of a successful system into another system design. If the design and function are clearly explained in the design documentation, the duplication is easy.

Systems crash. Good system specifications help people to bring them up again.

Who Writes a System Specification and Who Reads It?

The person who performs the lead system analyst function writes the system specification.

The primary reader is the programmer who builds the system's programs.

Secondary readers include those who may want to redesign the system—modify it, maintain it, duplicate it, or write system manuals. Any or all of these readers will need the system specification.

PART THREE DESIGN

Good Habits for Writing a Good System Specification

DOCUMENT CAREFULLY

Writers of system specifications must not assume they will remember what their scribbles mean or that others can decipher them. It is poor practice to document carelessly. It is also costly and aggravating to any person who must consult the design documentation in the future.

BE A VISIONARY

See the whole system as well as the parts. The overview lets the designer recognize interdependencies which cause the design to be logical, economical, and efficient.

FIT FORM TO FUNCTION

Mark out a design that allows the system to do what the functional specification says it must do.

BE GENEROUS

On a project that is at all sizable, a designer rarely works alone. Learn to be a good team worker. Allow others to make suggestions, accept good ideas, give credit to those who contribute, and delegate work.

RESPECT THE PROGRAMMER

When you design the system, you necessarily determine certain design specifications for programs. But remember your role. You are responsible for designing the total system. The programmer is responsible for designing individual programs. Do not infringe on the programmer's creativity and job.

DIVIDE AND CONQUER

Any large or complex system cannot be comprehended at one time. It must be broken apart and studied in units, then reassembled. The same approach is effective when writing. It makes the writing assignment seem less formidable, and it partitions the document itself. When carried over into document design, this partitioning breaks the document into units easy to refer to.

ORGANIZE AND OUTLINE

The parts of a system specification are fairly standard and normally include the following:

1. Identify the report and list its contents
2. Reintroduce the idea
3. Chart system information: flowcharts and data flow diagrams
4. Define data: dictionaries, files, records, and fields
5. Identify processing controls

6. Include program narratives
7. Explain operating characteristics
8. State restrictions and trade-offs
9. Show costs and schedules
10. Develop a system text plan

Most readers of the system specification are prepared to understand the report's technical information. Therefore, the writer's concern becomes how to organize this material so that the reader can use it efficiently and understand it accurately.

Knowing effective ways to present technical information is useful to people other than writers. One's ability to manage a writing project is partly tied to one's ability to offer constructive criticism. Being able to do this is a wonderful attribute of anyone in a position of authority because it helps others become better at their work.

1. Identify the Report and List its Contents

Everything said about this topic in Chapter 6, "Functional Specification I" applies also to this document. Use the information on page 93 to evaluate these examples.

EXAMPLES FOR SECTION 1: IDENTIFY THE REPORT
AND LIST ITS CONTENTS

Example 62

Compare the two examples that follow by judging 1. appearance, 2. effectiveness of title, and 3. completeness of information. Which example do you prefer? Why?

Title Page

Design Specifications

Voter Registration and
Jury Selection System of
Pinellas County

Jack Smart, Analyst I
Joseph Hodor, Analyst II
Peter Weaver, Analyst III

August 9, 1983

PART THREE   DESIGN

Table of Contents

```
System Flowchart ...................................... 1
File Definition ....................................... 2
Record Definition ..................................... 3
Field Definition ...................................... 4
Processing Controls ................................... 5
Program Narrative ..................................... 6
Operating Characteristics ............................. 7
Constraints ........................................... 8
Costs and Schedules ................................... 9
```

Example 63

Title Page

DESIGN SPECIFICATION
FOR
STUDENT REGISTRATION
AND
GRADE HANDLING SYSTEM

PREPARED FOR
GEORGETOWN COLLEGE
GEORGETOWN, MAINE

PREPARED BY
A. JANE SMITH, HEAD SYSTEMS ANALYST
B. JOSEPH BROWN, SYSTEMS ANALYST
C. FREDERICK THOMPSON, SYSTEMS ANALYST

THIS COMPLETELY ONLINE STUDENT REGISTRATION AND GRADE HANDLING SYSTEM WAS PREPARED IN RESPONSE TO A REQUEST BY DR. G. CONWAY, PRESIDENT OF GEORGETOWN COLLEGE ON AUGUST 1, 1983.

TABLE OF CONTENTS

SUBJECT	PAGE
GENERAL DESCRIPTION	1
SYSTEM FLOWCHART	2
FILE 1. STUDENT FILE	3
FILE 2. CLASS SCHEDULE FILE	7
PROCESSING CONTROLS	11
PROGRAM DESCRIPTIONS	
PROGRAM 1. CREATE/UPDATE CLASS SCHEDULE	13
PROGRAM 2. PRINT CLASS SCHEDULE	14
PROGRAM 3. CREATE/UPDATE STUDENT FILE	15
PROGRAM 4. ENROLL STUDENT (ADD/DROP)	16
PROGRAM 5. PRINT FACULTY CLASS LIST	17
PROGRAM 6. READ STUDENT GRADES	17
PROGRAM 7. PRINT STUDENT GRADE REPORTS	17
PROGRAM 8. PRINT STUDENT TRANSCRIPT STICKERS	17
OPERATING CHARACTERISTICS	18
ADVANTAGES OF PROPOSED SYSTEM	20
COST AND SCHEDULES	21
APPENDICES	22

COMMENT

Title Page: Both examples need improvement.

Example 62.

   Appearance: Too crowded. Distinguish title of document from title of system. (Put one in full caps or underline one.)
   Title: Too general. Say whether this is a system or program design specification.
   Completeness of Information: Incomplete. What firm do the analysts work for?

Example 63.

   Appearance: Everything too equal. Change some items from full caps. A complete sentence is not the best form for a title page. ("This completely online student . . .")
   Title: Good. It is specific.
   Completeness of Information: Incomplete. Did Mr. G. Conway make the request on August 1, 1983, or is this report being submitted on that date? What firm do the analysts work for?

Rewrite of Title Page for Example 63

ONLINE STUDENT AND GRADE HANDLING SYSTEM
FOR GEORGETOWN COLLEGE, GEORGETOWN, MAINE

System Specification

Prepared by Smith & Brown Data Consultants:
Jane Smith, Head System Analyst
Joseph Brown, System Analyst
Frederick Thompson, System Analyst

Submitted in response to request by Dr. G. Conway

Table of Contents: I prefer Example 63. It lists individual files and program descriptions so it is useful for reference.

2. Reintroduce the Idea: Again Please!

Introduce the reader to the report again so the two can interact. If a report just begins, reading it is like coming into the middle of a discussion. At first you try to figure out what is being said, but if that proves too difficult, you lose interest and do not care about knowing the topic or the people talking. The same applies to "meeting" a document. In order to contribute, the programmer or anyone else reading the system specification needs to know why this system is being designed and what it is to do.

EXAMPLES FOR SECTION 2: REINTRODUCE THE IDEA

Example 64

Imagine coming to a system specification just as you are reading this example. You are the program designer, but you have no prior knowledge of this system which is your next project. You pick up the report and see this title page.

Title Page

>   Design Specifications
>
>   Voter Registration and
>   Jury Selection System of
>   Pinellas County
>
>
>   Jack Smart, Analyst I
>   Joseph Hodor, Analyst II
>   Peter Weaver, Analyst III
>
>
>   August 9, 1983

You open to the table of contents and glance over it.

>   Table of Contents
>
>   System Flowchart 1
>   File Definition 2
>   Record Definition 3
>   Field Definition 4
>   Processing Controls 5
>   Program Narrative 6
>   Operating Characteristics 7
>   Constraints 8
>   Cost and Schedules 9

You turn the page and see this.

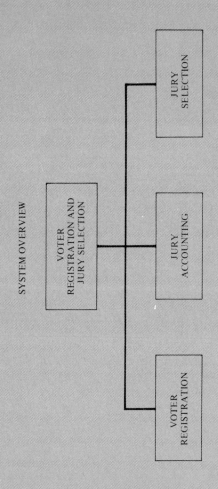

COMMENT
1. I see no need for the System Overview to be printed sideways.
2. What is the System Overview? Why am I reading it? What is it supposed to be illustrating or explaining to me?
3. Is the System Overview on page 1? The page is not numbered. If it is page 1, I am puzzled to find that the Table of Contents lists "System Flowchart" for page 1. Are the two the same? Be consistent.
4. I want to quit and will if I can or, at least, take a coffee break. I am not interested because no effort has been made to introduce me or draw me into the report. All effort to be a part of the report and to contribute is left up to me.

Example 65

Consider this page, which follows a title page and table of contents of a system specification for a physician's accounting package. How well does this introduction inform the reader, make him or her familiar with the document, and prepare the reader to participate?

```
                    SYSTEM FLOWCHARTS
In order to see what the accounting system being developed for
Dr. X will do, the following diagrams will be presented in this
section:
    1. Overall structure chart of the entire system
    2. System flowchart

Structure Chart
The overall structure chart of the system is presented on page
2. This structure chart illustrates the major program modules
and the ordering in which each may be involved. All of these
modules are described in detail in the Automated Operations
section.

System Flowchart
The system flowchart is presented on pages 3 and 4. This flow-
chart illustrates
    1. How individual modules and processes of the system are
       related.
    2. The flow of data through the system.
    3. The following four files that are used in the system:
        1. Patient Account File              (PATIENT.DAT)
        2. Reorganized Patient Acct. File    (PAT.DAT)
        3. Delinquent Acct. File             (DELIN.DAT)
        4. Reorganized Del. Acct. File       (DEL.DAT)
```

PART THREE DESIGN

COMMENT
The intent and information seem proper. I understand that the system is an accounting system for a single individual and that the charts will explain the system's functions. I like being told what I will be reading. However the presentation both in format and language needs attention.

I suggest changing the format in order to use a formal outline hierarchy to present and separate information:

I.
  A.
    1.
      a.

This outline hierarchy will eliminate the ineffective use of 1, 2, 3 to number everything.

Make items parallel. For example, present the information under "Structure Chart" and "System Flowchart" in the same way. Always call items by the same name. Capitalize consistently. Tighten language. See rewrite for constructive changes.

Rewrite

System Charts

~~The following charts show what~~ The potential for the Accounting System being developed for Dr. X ~~will do.~~ is illustrated in the following charts: [language tightened]

The introductory sentences following I and II now match. The outline hierarchy of I, A, 1, makes corresponding parts easier to see.

I. Overall Structure Chart

II. System Flowchart

Capitalization consistent and Titles made consistent throughout

I. (Overall Structure Chart) → *Items now named the same and capitalized alike*

The (Overall Structure Chart) is presented on page 2. The ~~Structure~~ **S**tructure chart illustrates: [language tightened]

  A. Major program modules

  B. Order in which each may be invoked

All ~~of these~~ modules are described in detail in the Automated Operations Section (see page 16).

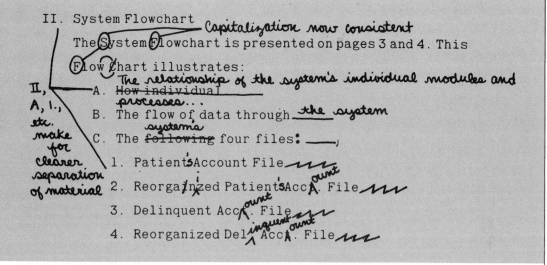

Example 66

This page follows a title page and table of contents. How comfortable do you feel beginning to read the document? How well have you been introduced?

```
                    GENERAL DESCRIPTION
The online system will facilitate, speed up, and increase the
efficiency of:
     A. Class Schedule Production
     B. Student Registration
        1. Counselor access to class schedule
        2. Counselor access to student information
        3. Counselor enrollment of student
        4. Registrar add/drop process
     C. Faculty Class List Production
     D. Grade Handling Procedure
        1. Grade list reading
        2. Student grade report production
        3. Student transcript sticker production
```

COMMENT
The material comes too quickly. First, I need a statement of the problem and what the system must achieve. Then I could understand the need to "facilitate," "speed up," and "increase efficiency."

PART THREE DESIGN

Example 67

Consider this introduction to a system specification for an informed retrieval project. It follows a title page and table of contents. How might you format better and tighten the language?

> I. INTRODUCTION
>
> ICM has found it necessary to make data available to its sales persons concerning products it has sold or leased, businesses and locations of businesses to whom these products are sold or leased, applications which these businesses are making of the products, cost of the products, installation and sales dates, and peripheral equipment associated with the main product line.
>
> This information, or selected parts of it, is requested by customers and is to be used by salespeople to help them increase sales through better customer satisfaction.
>
> The system is designed and intended to make the salesperson's task in obtaining this information as easy as possible by using a series of queries to solicit the information the salesperson wants.
>
> To serve the function of making the information accessible and accurate, the query and help utility must access the most accurate and current master file of data, which in turn shall be updated, backed up, and reports generated for managerial understanding and control.

COMMENT

Informing the reader of the purpose for proposing and designing the system is good.

The document could be formatted better and words could be cut. See the edited revision.

Rewrite

[Handwritten edits:]

Numbers separate the information for easy reading and referencing

Introduction

ICM has found ~~it necessary to make data available to its sales~~ that its salespersons need the following data: [rewritten to be direct]

~~persons concerning:~~ 1) products ICM ~~it~~ has sold or leased; 2) businesses and location of businesses who bought or leased these ~~to whom those~~ products;

are sold or leased; 3) applications which these businesses are making of the products; 4) cost of the products; 5) installation and sales dates; and 6) peripheral equipment associated with the main product line.

Salespersons select parts of the information, or selected parts of it, is requested by customers and is used by salespeople to help them increase sales through better customer satisfaction.

The system's designed and intended to make the salesperson's task in obtaining this information as easy as possible by using a series of queries to solicit the information the salesperson wants.

(margin notes: rewritten to active voice; The rewrite uses active voice and more direct statements; Possessives correctly used)

Example 68

The example is an introduction to system specification for a nonprinted call card analysis system. This writing is simple and clear. It tells enough without going into great detail. The tone is formal. It is a good model.

The Alpha Beta Ceta (ABC) Sales Call System was developed to aid in monitoring and improving the performance functions and activities of the sales force. It provides sales representatives with two preprinted call cards for each key client on the representative's scheduled contact list. In addition, each representative has blank (non-preprinted) call cards to fill out when he or she contacts a client who has no preprinted card.

However, the current Sales Call System possesses no extension, either manual or automated, which analyzes non-preprinted call card data. Once non-preprinted call data are edited and keyed, they are merged with the preprinted call file and all data unique to the non-preprinted call cards are lost to the system.

> A study of the call cards received during Period II, 1982 revealed that approximately 25,000 non-preprinted cards were used compared to approximately 140,000 preprinted cards. The high number of non-preprinted call cards being returned makes it necessary to develop a means to analyze non-preprinted call card data in an effort to reduce the number used and to provide better information to the sales representative.

3. Chart System Information: System Flowcharts and Data Flow Diagrams

Charts picture system information so the reader has an overview. This perspective helps in problem solving, for it permits the viewer to see at one time the system as a whole.

The "picture" cannot be a drawing that only the designer understands. Instead, it must use conventional symbols that let others who know these symbols read the chart and understand it correctly.

Charts have both immediate and future use. During the time of original design, the system designer and the program designer use charts to plot their design, to record the system's network of processes and procedures, and to reveal its logic. The act of creating the charts forces the designers to consider the whole system. They cannot skip over or delay dealing with tough problems.

Later, charts are used by anyone returning to maintain, modify, or imitate the system. They are its hieroglyphs. Translating their symbols reveals the system's origin.

The following rules apply generally to drawing effective charts:

1. Use standard symbols.
2. If symbols must be created, provide a key.
3. Name everything correctly and usefully.
4. Identify each chart and page: system's title, author's name, date of preparation, page number.
5. Format the page. Fit the chart to the space. Make the page attractive and easy to read.
6. Partition the chart into subcharts when the whole system cannot be shown on a single page.
7. Keep direction flow consistent—either vertical or horizontal.
8. Use the same size paper for all charts in a series.
9. Indicate whether a process is performed daily, weekly, monthly, or as required.

8 SYSTEM SPECIFICATION I · 143

TWO CHARTS COMMON IN SYSTEM SPECIFICATION

A. System Flowcharts: A system flowchart pictures the physical system. Each symbol represents a component. The chart illustrates the flow of data among the components and shows the way data are stored and processed among those components.

Uses of a System Flowchart: A flowchart allows the reader to visualize how the system will be implemented. It condenses into one chart a system in which processes may occur at different times, in several buildings, and over a number of days or weeks. Managers and/or clients can anticipate the costs and changes necessary to implement the system.

A flowchart becomes a reference. Whenever one needs to understand how a separate component fits into the whole, the flowchart shows this; whenever one needs to ask again what happens to certain data before or after they arrive at this juncture, the flowchart shows this.

The *basic flowchart symbols* to use when designing are given below and on the next page.

Symbol	Name	Symbol	Name
▭	Process	⌭	Magnetic disk
▱	Input/output	⌬	Magnetic drum
○	Connector	⬠	Display
⬠	Off-page connector	▰	Manual input
▽	Merge	◇	Decision
→	Flowline		
○	Magnetic tape		

PART   THREE DESIGN

Online storage

Punched card

Document

Sort

Manual operation

Auxiliary operation

Communication link

Basic Rules for Designing Flowcharts
Apply the rules common to charting (p. 142).
Use one symbol for each system component.
Label each symbol.
Partition the chart if system is complicated or large. Show major components on the introductory chart; show individual components on a separate chart.
Use an off-page connector symbol if the flowchart is more than one page or if it is partitioned.

EXAMPLES FOR SECTION 3: SYSTEM FLOWCHARTS

Example 69

Consider this system flowchart for an information retrieval project and check your ideas with mine.

8   SYSTEM SPECIFICATION I   145

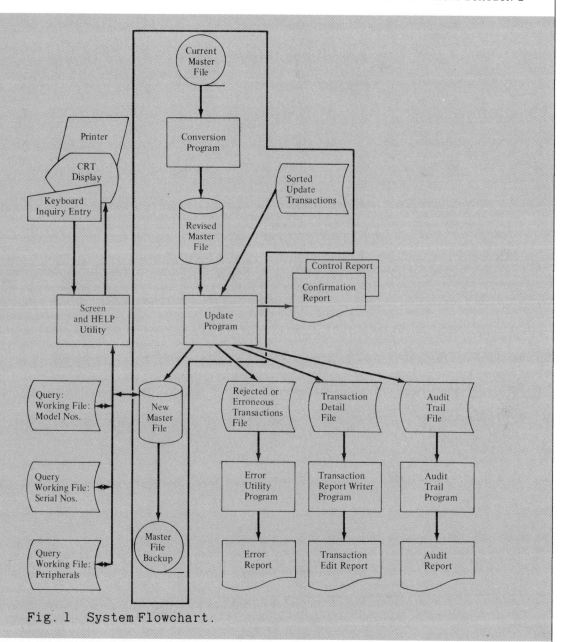

Fig. 1   System Flowchart.

COMMENT
1. Good format: the chart fills the page well.
2. Each symbol is clearly labeled.
3. Flow is in one direction—top to bottom.
4. Standard symbols are used.
5. The chart reads precisely and, we will assume, correctly.

146 PART THREE DESIGN

Suggested Improvements

Title the chart specifically. Name the system; add the designer's name, date of preparation.

Process descriptions should explain at what point a process is performed (if applicable).

Example 70

Practice in translating: Read the symbols on the flowchart at the left side of the page. Compare your reading to mine. If they are similar, we know that the designer has created a chart that communicates well.

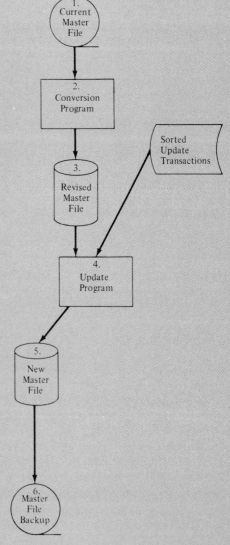

1. Your reading: _____

   My reading: Transactions enter the system from a current master file which is on magnetic tape.

2. Your reading: _____

   My reading: Transactions are processed by a conversion program.

3. Your reading: _____

   My reading: Conversion program revises the Master File on magnetic disk.

4. Your reading: _____

   My reading: The revised Master File and the sorted update transactions are both processed by the update program.

5. Your reading: _____

   My reading: A new Master File is available on magnetic disk.

6. Your reading: _____

   My reading: A Master File backup exists on magnetic tape.

Example 71

What rules does the designer follow in creating this chart? What improvements do you suggest?

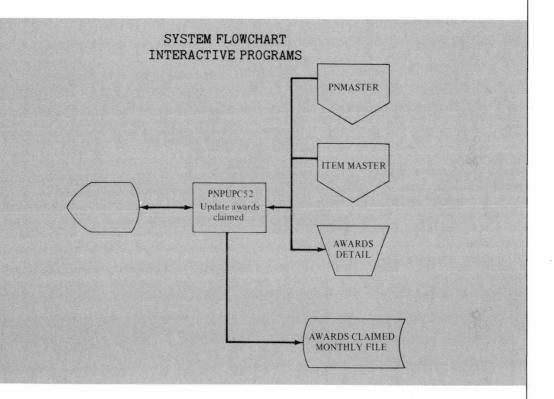

COMMENT

Good Points

Moves in one direction; uses standard symbols; labels symbols; fits page satisfactorily.

Suggested Improvements

Identify system's name and designer's name; label the ⬠ symbol.

Substitute a standard symbol for the nonstandard symbol

or identify it.

Example 72

How successful do you judge this system flowchart and its use of the off-page connector?

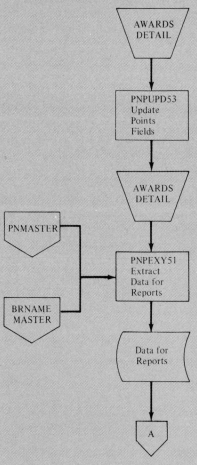

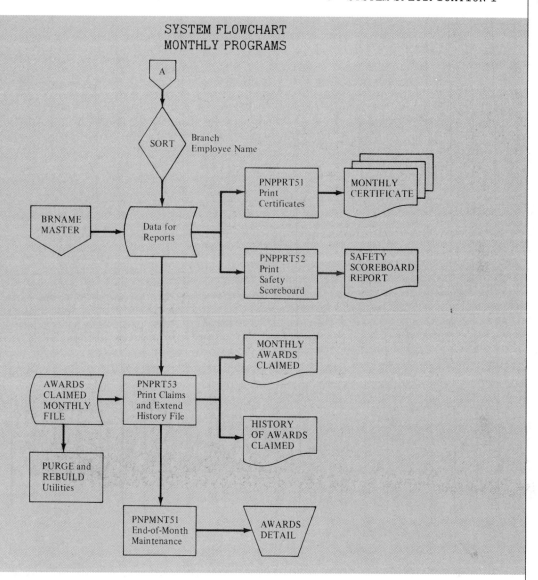

COMMENT
Use the following questions to guide your evaluation.
    How well are items named?
    How effective is the format?
    How consistent is the flow?
    How clear is the partitioning?
    How effective is the use of the connector?
    How clearly are the processes identified?
    How well are you able to visualize the system?
    How well do you understand when a process is performed?
    Are the symbols used standard ones?

PART THREE DESIGN

PRACTICE IN READING SYSTEM FLOWCHARTS

Example 73

Read with me the following section of the chart in Example 72. Do we agree? If not, what are the problems? Are they in the design of the chart? What could be changed to make the reading more accurate? If we agree, the designer has drawn the chart well.

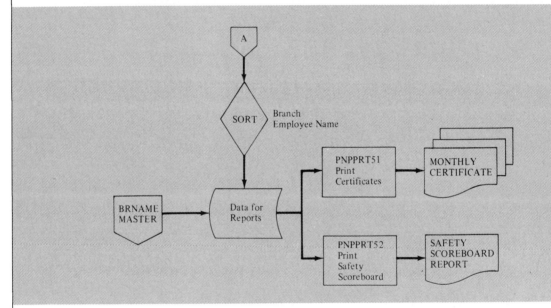

COMMENT

My Chart Reading

　Data for reports are received online from a branch name master file and from a sorting of branch employee names. (The source of names is a file not shown on this page.)
　The data for reports is processed by either the print certificates program or the print safety scoreboard program.
　Documents are printed out for each program: monthly certificates and a safety scoreboard report.

Example 74

Compare your evaluation of this system flowchart for a student registration and grade handling system with my comments.

8 SYSTEM SPECIFICATION I 151

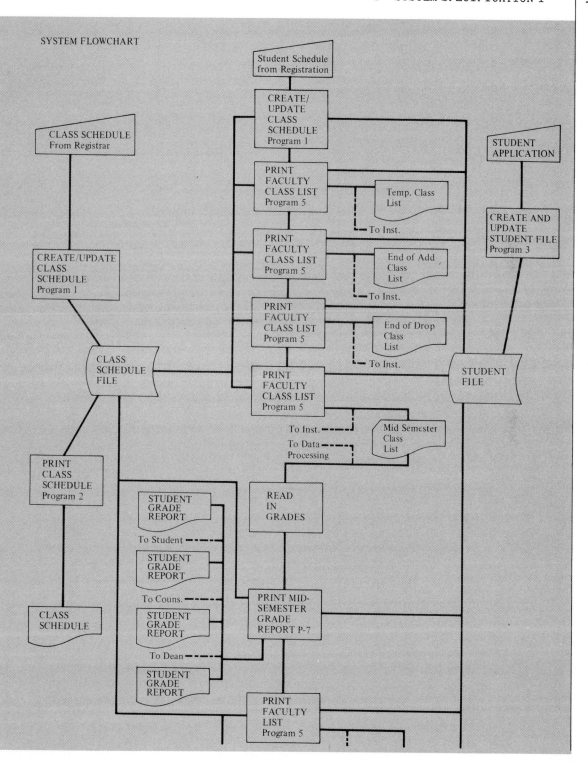

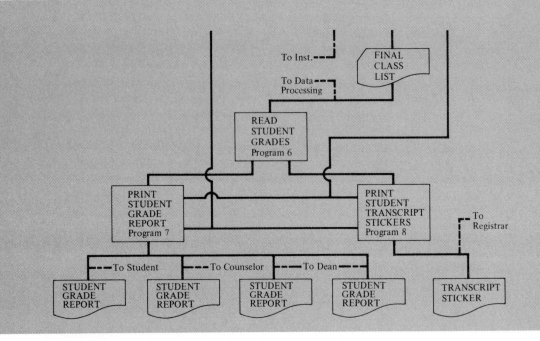

COMMENT

The chart fails because of one major omission; no arrows show flow of data. In addition, the chart should either be redesigned so it fits on one page, or it should show the main components on one page and partition the details.

The chart is very dense and appears formidable. An introduction would help the reader get started.

B. Data Flow Diagrams: A data flow diagram pictures how data are used, moved, and changed as they "flow" through the system. The chart is not concerned with hardware, software, files, or anything physical. Its only concern is a logical model of data flow.

Uses of a Data Flow Diagram: The system designer uses this chart to organize data collected during system analysis, and to show how the present processes for data work, how the proposed system must function, and how the data are related to each other.

The nontechnical user can read the diagram and thereby participate in the system development because of the simplicity of this diagram (it uses only four symbols) and its subject matter (data). The more the user can understand, approve, suggest, and alter, the more effective the system will be.

The designer uses the data flow diagram as a check sheet for developing the system's files and programs, retracing data, and checking that no data have been omitted or directed to the wrong component.

Rules for Designing Data Flow Diagrams
Apply the rules common to charting (p. 142).
When possible, show the flow of data from its source in the upper left of the page to its destination in the lower right.
Use basic data flow diagram symbols:

Source of destination of data   □

Process that transforms data   □ or ○

Data store   ▭

Data flow   →

EXAMPLES FOR SECTION 3: DATA FLOW DIAGRAMS

Example 75

After comparing the following two examples, Example 75A appears better than Example 75B. My comments written on the charts themselves explain my preference. Do you agree? What can you add?

154 PART THREE DESIGN

APPENDIX B

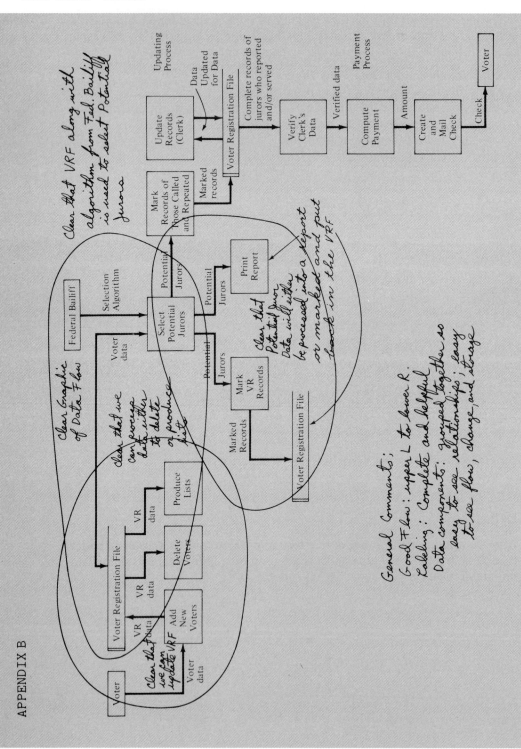

8 SYSTEM SPECIFICATION I 155

APPENDIX B

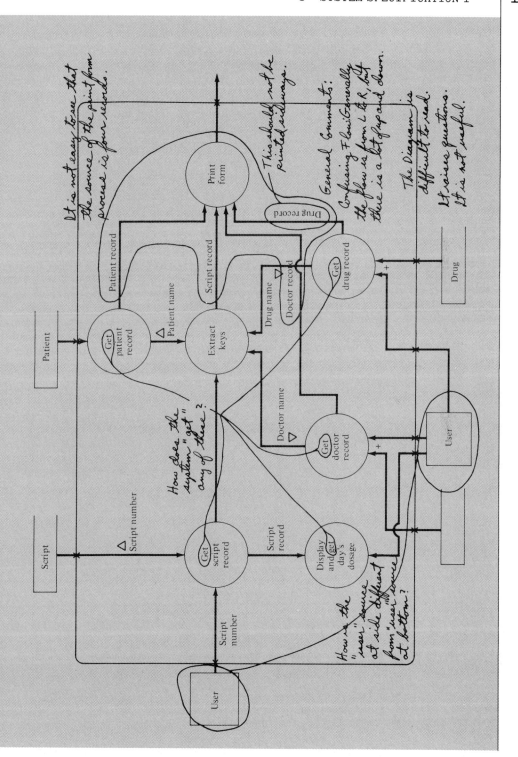

Example 76

The following example is effective. Example 76A clearly pictures data flow and shows how data are related to each other. Example 76B illustrates how data in a single process moves and changes.

The main disadvantage of these examples is that multiple pages are used to picture data flow. (One page illustrates each process.) It is easier to see and evaluate a diagram that is on one page, but this disadvantage is offset here by the detail and clarity of the data presented.

Example 76A

See the opposite page.

8   SYSTEM SPECIFICATION I

Example 76A

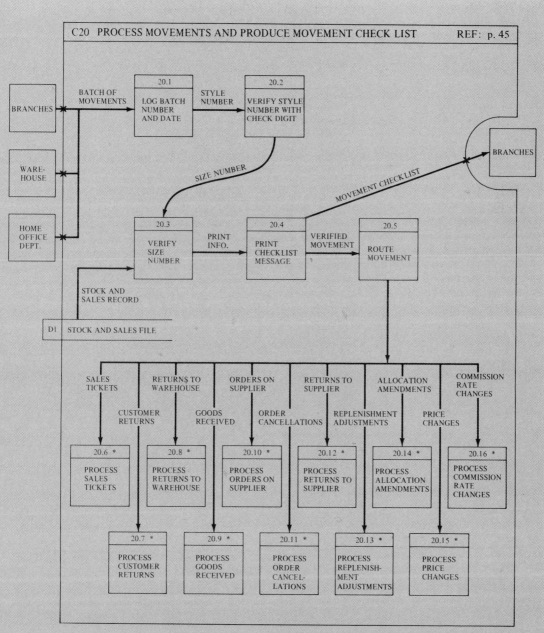

PART THREE DESIGN

Example 76B

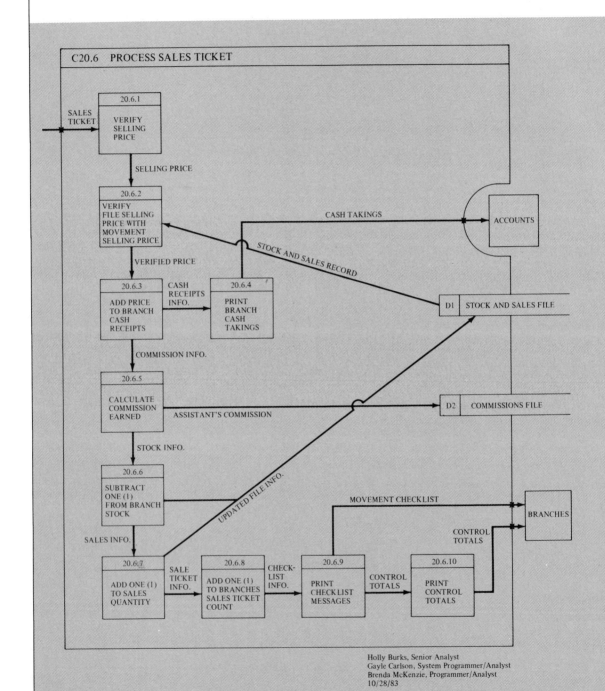

CHECKLIST: CHAPTER 8
System Specification I

DEFINITION	Serves as the system's major technical document.
FUNCTION	Serves as a reference for building programs, as the source for the operations manual, and as the origin of future system modification.
WRITER	Lead system analyst.
AUDIENCE	Programmer, writer of systems' manuals, and anyone else who redesigns system.
GOOD WORK HABITS	Document carefully. Be a visionary. See the whole system as well as its parts. Fit form to function. Be generous. Allow others to contribute. Respect the programmer. Do not infringe on his or her work. Divide and conquer. Partition the work.
OUTLINE	
1. IDENTIFY THE REPORT AND LIST ITS CONTENTS	See information on p. 93.
2. REINTRODUCE THE IDEA	State why the system is being designed and state its purpose so a reader can effectively read this document.
3. CHART SYSTEM INFORMATION: FLOWCHARTS AND DATA FLOW DIAGRAMS	Use conventional symbols. Provide a key. Name everything correctly and usefully. Identify each chart and page. Give system's title, author's name, date of preparation, and page number. Format and fit chart to space. Partition chart into subcharts when system is too large to picture on one page. Use the same size paper for a series of charts. Keep direction flow consistent. Indicate if a process is performed daily, weekly, monthly, etc.
A. FLOWCHARTS	Pictures the physical system. Shows the flow of data among the components. Condenses a system into one chart. Serves as a reference for anyone needing to understand how a part of the system fits into the whole.

PART THREE DESIGN

          Design Rules:
              Use basic symbols. See pp. 143–144.
              Use one symbol for each component.
              Label each symbol.
              Partition the chart if the system is complicated.
              Use an off-page connector symbol if the chart is more than one page.

B. DATA FLOW DIAGRAMS — Pictures how data are used, moved, and changed.
Organizes collected data. Shows how present processed data work, how the proposed system must function, and how data relate.

          Design Rules:
              Use basic symbols. See p. 153.
              Apply rules listed for charting. See this checklist.

9
System Specification II

4. Define Data: Dictionaries, Files, Records, and Fields

Defining is a major part of writing a system specification. The common denominator of all definitions is data. The data dictionary, files, records, and fields—individually and collectively—explain the purpose, content, and layout of the data that belong to the whole system and to individual files. The definitions become the building material for constructing the rest of the system.

DATA DICTIONARY

The primary element in the collection of four definitions is the data dictionary, a file that defines all data items, records, and files used within a system.

The compilation of the data dictionary for a sizable system is an arduous task, but its value makes the work worthwhile. The dictionary sets accepted meanings for the context of the system; it provides the language consistency that improves accuracy and communication. It cross-references data. When any modification to data is necessary, the dictionary lists all other programs, files, and systems that use the same data. This source of data is immensely useful when you need to know what other programs or forms use the same data.

A data dictionary is a necessity for the programmer. It gives the programmer a set of authorized definitions to use when creating modules, programs, and even systems that must link or interface.

With a data dictionary, the programmer does not have to duplicate the work of defining when designing each program, adding to an existing system, or designing a new interdependent system. He or she can avoid making multiple definitions for identical items in systems belonging to the same organization.

If a system is large or if more than one programmer works on it, a data dictionary is essential. Otherwise the same item may be known by different names in different programs.

Tips for Designing a Good Data Dictionary: One practical way to compile data information is to use cards. During system development, record information on individual cards. When the system design is complete, shuffle and organize the cards to write the dictionary. Alphabetize the entries.

Make definitions consistent and accurate. Include basic information for each entry:

Data name
Aliases
Description
Format
Location
Notes

EXAMPLES FOR SECTION 4: DATA DICTIONARY

Example 77

This excerpt, from a data dictionary for a system to solve linear programming problems, is not effective. Determine why.

DATA DICTIONARY

HUE—The color value for graphing constraints
I—Constraint #—Index for arrays
I1INTERSECT—Temporary value used to find extreme points
I2INTERSECT—Temporary value used to find extreme points
J—Temporary value for array index

COMMENT
This item is misnamed. It is a collection of information, but not a data dictionary. Label documents and parts of documents accurately and traditionally. Whenever a standard definition, title, or form exists use it. This practice will encourage the standardization needed in computer documentation.

Example 78

The information in this data dictionary for a Pharmacy Information System is not standard. The writer adds information that is beyond the intent of a data dictionary. For example, the input/output information begins to show how the data is used. A data dictionary should just define data, not explain its use.

DATA DICTIONARY

Variables used as parameters of global variables but excluding local work variables:

VARIABLE NAME	DESCRIPTION	INPUT PARAMETER TO	OUTPUT PARAMETER FROM
AB (flag)	Flag to abort Process Script	New script Refill script	Collect records
AN (flag)	Flag to add drug record to file	Add new info to files New script Refill script	Collect records New script Refill script
CH$	Coded Price	New script Refill script Print label Add info to files	Code price New script Refill script

Example 79

This excerpt, from a data dictionary for PSAT Student Recruiting System, is a good model.

DATA DICTIONARY

How to Read the Data Dictionary

Data Name	Information name for general reference. NOT to be used in programs
Data Length	Character length of information
Bytes Required	Number of bytes needed to store information
Dept. Responsible for Entry	Department that enters and updates information

Record Segment Code	Tells which line of 100 bytes the information found on. Located along left side of record layout
Field Code	Name used in programs when referencing the information
Field Location	Exact place in file information is located
Data Specifications	Detailed instruction about information; how it is coded in file

Page 1.

Data Name	College code
Data Length	8
Bytes Required	8
Dept. Responsible for Entry	Admissions office
Record Segment Code	0
Field Code	School
Field Location	1–8
Data Specifications	University's code is 00120801

COMMENT

The dictionary informs the reader. It uses a standardized form, one that could easily be duplicated and used by everyone in a particular shop. The definitions are precise, complete, and useful to programming and storing. The assigning of responsibility ("Dept. Responsible for Entry") is excellent.

FILES, RECORDS, AND FIELDS

The three together complete a file definition and have their own step-down structure:

The file definition identifies the name, purpose, content, and format of a group of related records.
The record definition identifies the name, content, and format of a group of related fields that make up a file.
The field definition identifies the name, content, and format of data times that make up a record.

These definitions are essential to the program designer at this stage and to anyone needing to understand how the data works in the future.

9 SYSTEM SPECIFICATION II   165

Tips for Designing File/Record/Field Definitions: Explain the purpose of the files and the purpose of records within a file.

Tell why the file design was chosen.

When possible, picture the information. Use a preprinted form or create a standard way to present information.

Define by using standard items:
  File Definition
    File Name
    Origin
    Preceding job step (or other source if outside system)
    Destination (next job step—if external, recipient)
    Fixed/variable format
    Type of label
    File organization
    Access method
    Sequence
    Block length
    Medium
    Estimated volume
    Backup and retention instructions
    File structure
    Name of records in file
  Record Definition
    Name of record
    Name of associated file
    Fixed/variable format
    Length in bytes
    Sequence of specific records
    Record identifier
  Field Definition
    Name of field
    Usage
    Size of field in bytes
    Format of field
    Edit requirement
    Source

Note: Not every data item applies to every definition. The designer must decide which are applicable. If you suspect a question may arise, show the item and comment that it is not applicable.

EXAMPLES FOR SECTION 4: FILES, RECORDS, FIELDS

Example 80

Compare the following two examples. Each has a contrasting strength and weakness. Decide what you think they are.

Example 80A

This is an excerpt from Voter Registration and Jury Selection System.

FILE DEFINITION

    Name: Voter Registration
    Type of Label: Standard System
    Origin: External, from Voter Registration Cards; Updates, from Selection Process
    Format: Fixed
    File Organization: ISAM
    Access Method: Sequential
    Block Length: 512 Bytes
    Estimated Volume: 90,000–100,000 Records, 256 bytes each.

RECORD DEFINITION

    Name of Record: Voter
    Name of File: Voter Registration
    Format: Fixed
    Identifier: Voter Registration Number
    Length: 256 Bytes (see Field Definitions)

FIELD DEFINITIONS

Character fields will be stored one character/byte. Numeric values will be stored in zoned decimal format.

OPR	3 alpha characters	Initials of person entering data on screen
REG NO.	1 alpha character 1–5 digits	Identification of the registrant in alpha-numeric form
NAME	36 alpha characters 19 alpha characters 17 alpha characters	First and middle name Last name

COMMENT

Good Points

The form for file and record definitions is excellent. It lends itself to duplication and to creating a standard in-house form.

Suggestion

Set items like "name" (under "File Definition") and "type of label" in full caps.

Things to Improve

The field definitions are weak because they are difficult to reference. One must count to find where an item appears. For example, the last name of a person begins in position 28. The only way to know that is to count $3 + 1 + 5 + 19 = 28$.

Suggestion

Label the three columns used in "Field Definitions" and add one other titled "Relative Position."

The information in the three columns is not identified. It should be. Why is standard information—Usage? Format?—omitted?

Example 80B

This is an excerpt from a Pharmacy Information System.

```
File Design
    1. Doctor File
        A. D-index
            Index file for doctors
            Sequential access by doctor's last name
            Doctor number field points to doctor file
            Record length: 35 bytes
            File size: up to 150 records
```

D-INDEX RECORD FORMAT

DOCTOR NAME	CR	DOCTOR NUMBER	CR
0 DN $ 29	30 31	DN 34	35

```
        B. Doctor
            Data file for doctors
            Random access by doctor number
            Pointed to by doctor number field of D-Index
```

Record length: 109 bytes
File size: up to 150 records

DOCTOR RECORD FORMAT

DN$	DA$	DC$	DS$	DZ$	DP$	DD$	DM$
NAME	STREET ADDRESS	CITY	STATE	ZIP	PH. NO.	IDEA NO.	MEDICAID NO.
0　　29	30　　　　　59	60　　79	80　81	82　86	87　　96	97　103	104　　　108

C. Field Descriptions
```
    DN$: Doctor's name (Last First MI)              30 Alpha
    DN : Doctor number. Pointer to Doctor File      3 digits
    DA$: Doctor's street address                    30 Alpha
    DC$: Doctor's city                              20 Alpha
    DS$: Doctor's state abbreviation                 2 Alpha
    DZ$: Doctor's zip code                           5 Alpha
    DP$: Doctor's phone number (nnnnnnnnnn)         10 Alpha
    DD$: Doctor's DEA number (nnnnnnn)               7 Alpha
    DM$: Doctor's Medicaid provider number           5 Alpha
```

COMMENT

Good Points: Picturing the record format is good.

Things to Improve: The description of data is weak. No headings are used to identify items. For example, under "1. Doctor File" what are the "D-index," and "Index file for doctors"? The reader can only guess or run through in his or her mind possible items and try to fit these items to one.

Example 81

The format of this example from a physicians's accounting package system makes the information easy to read. Numbering the positions will make it even better (see unshaded numbers). The example appears to merge "File," "Record," and "Field" definitions. Why do this? Why not divide the three and present each separately?

FILE NAME: Delinquent Account File

DATA ITEM	DESCRIPTION	LENGTH
1. PTNAMES$	name of patient	40 characters
2. PTADDR1$	street address of patient	40 characters
3. PTADDR2$	city and state of patient	31 characters
4. PRZIP$	patient zip code	9 digits
5. SSNO$	social security number	11 digits
6. AMOUNT	amount of or cost of service	7 digits
7. SERDATE$	date of service	8 characters
8. CURBAL	current balance (amt. owed)	7 digits

MAXIMUM RECORD SIZE FOR FILE: 153 characters
STORAGE DEVICE: IBM Personal Computer disk drive
MEDIUM: Diskette

Sample Fields:

```
S T U A R T , _ A N N _ W _ _ _ _ _ _ _ _ _ _ _ _ _ _ _ _ _ _ _ _ _ _ _ _ _ _ _ _ _ _ _ _ _ _ _ _ _
1   ---patient name                                                                            40

8 0 2 _ E I G H T H _ S T R E E T _ _ _ _ _ _ _ _ _ _ _ _ _ _ _ _ _ _ _ _ _ _ _ _ _ _
41  ---street address of patient                                                               80

E V A N S V I L L E , _ I N _ _ _ _ _ _ _ _ _ _ _ _ _ _ _ _ _ _
81  ---city and state of patient                                 111

3 3 2 1 0 _ _ _ _   zip code of patient
112         120

4 0 0 - 6 3 - 0 8 0 8   social security number
121               131

1 0 0 0 0 . 0 0   amount or cost of service
132       138

0 3 1 1 9 1 8 3   date of service
139       146

1 0 0 0 0 . 0 0   current balance (amt. owed)
147       153
```

Example 82

The following example supports my preference for standarized forms. Notice how clearly the field and record definitions appear and how effectively information is "pictured."

170 PART THREE DESIGN

DASD/TAPE RECORD LAYOUT
NOTES---COMMENTS

APPLICATION	OUT-PATIENT
RECORD NAME	OPBLMST
DATE ORIGINATED	
REVISION DATE	

ANALYST PROGRAMMER	
RECORD SIZE	510
BLOCK SIZE	4080
RECORDS PER BLOCK	8
REVISION NUMBER	
VOLUME ID	

RECORDING MODE: FIXED ■ VAR ☐ UNDEF ☐ SPAN ☐
LABEL RECORDS: STANDARD ■ OMITTED ☐
ORGANIZATION TYPE: SAM ■ VSAM ☐ ISAM ☐ DAM ☐
RETENTION:

(Record layout grid, positions 01–250, with fields:)

- 01–50: PATIENT NAME / STREET / PATIENT CITY / PATIENT STATE / PATIENT ZIP / PATIENT NUMBER / PATNO / ENDING SERVICE DATE / BIRTH DAY / SOCIAL SECURITY NUMBER / SUFFIX / MEDICAL ID NUMBER / MEDI-CAL
- 51–100: BLUE CROSS PLAN NO. / KAISER FOREMP PLAN / RELATIVE FLAGS / FILLER / JOB / MEMBER'S NAME / DOCTOR'S CITY, STATE, ZIP / DR MED NO. PREFIX / DOCTORS MEDICAL NUMBER / RELATIONSHIP / NO DOCTOR / FILLER / DATE OF ACCIDENT / TIME OF ACCIDENT (HHMM) / TO / DOCTOR'S NAME / ACCIDENT TIME / TEMP / PULSE / VISIT / 5999949
- 101–150: INSURANCE BILL TO CITY / INSURANCE BILL TO NAME / BILL TO STATE / BILL TO ZIP CODE / POLICY NUMBER / PT. SEX MAR STA / GROUP NUMBER / INSURANCE BILL TO STREET / DIAGNOSIS 1
- 201–: INSURANCE BILL TO CITY

FIELD CONT. ☒ (repeated)

DATA-NAME (repeated)

Example 83

Parts of this example are good. Decide which parts you think are effective and determine why.

```
                Student Registration and Grade Handling System
FILE 1: STUDENT FILE

FILE DEFINITION TO FILE 1.

    A. NAME OF FILE: Student File
    B. TYPE OF LABEL: Omitted
    C. ORIGIN OF FILE:
        1. Jobs that access and modify file
            a. Enroll student (add/drop)
            b. Create/update student file
            c. Read student grades
        2. Jobs that access file only
            a. Print student grade reports
            b. Print student transcript stickers
            c. Print faculty class list
    D. FORMAT OF FILE: Variable
    E. ORGANIZATION OF FILE: Direct (key: Student Number)
    F. METHOD OF ACCESS: Random
    G. LENGTH OF BLOCK
        1. Minimum: 138 words
        2. Maximum: 429 words
    H. VOLUME OF FILE: 4000 records
    I. NAME OF RECORD: Student Information Record
    J. BACKUP OF FILE
        1. On magnetic tape
        2. For details, see page 11

RECORD DEFINITION OF FILE 1
    A. NAME OF RECORD: Student Information Record
    B. NAME OF FILE: Student File
    C. FORMAT OF RECORD: Variable
    D. IDENTIFIER OF RECORD: Student Number (5 characters)
    E. LENGTH OF RECORD:
        1. Bytes
            a. Minimum: 275
            b. Maximum: 740
        2. Words
            a. Minimum: 138
            b. Maximum: 370
```

```
FIELD DEFINITIONS OF RECORD OF FILE 1

FIELD (1) OF RECORD OF FILE 1
     A. NAME OF FIELD: Student Name
     B. SIZE OF FIELD: 25 bytes
     C. DATA TYPE OF FIELD: Character
     D. FORMAT OF FIELD: Alphabetic
     E. EDIT REQUIREMENTS OF FIELD: Non-blank

FIELD (2) OF RECORD OF FILE 1
     A. NAME OF FIELD: Student Number
     B. SIZE OF FIELD: 5 Bytes
     C. DATA TYPE OF FIELD: Character
     D. FORMAT OF FIELD: Numeric
     E. EDIT REQUIREMENTS OF FIELD
        1. Numeric
        2. Range (00000-99999)
        3. Non-blank

FIELD (3)
(The descriptions continue in this way.)
```

COMMENT
1. The format for file and record definitions is excellent.
2. The capitalization effectively separates item name from description.
3. The information is complete and standard; when an item does not apply, it is listed and entered as "omitted."
4. The field definitions however are cumbersome. You have to work too hard to get the information you need. Who wants to go through A, B, C, D, E for every field? Draw a picture.

Example 84

This file, record, field definition is a good example. The designer lays out the data pictorially, but at the same time gives a complete verbal description of every field. This format becomes a great convenience for the programmer. He or she can begin work efficiently and easily.

ACCOUNTS FILE

FILE DESCRIPTION: The Accounts File will contain data concerning customer transactions, addresses and discounts. The file will contain one record for each of Duell's three hundred customers.

RECORD DESCRIPTION: The records are fixed length records of 719 characters.

RECORD LAYOUT:

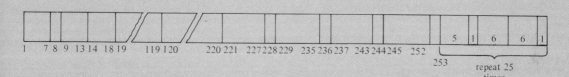

NAME: Account Number
FORMAT: Numeric
SIZE: 7 digits
LOCATION IN RECORD: Bytes 1 through 7
DESCRIPTION: Each number is unique made up of branch code, group number, and record number.

NAME: Class of Multiple Account
FORMAT: Numeric
SIZE: 1 digit
LOCATION IN RECORD: Byte 8
DESCRIPTION: This indicates location invoices and statements are sent to. The value must be a 1, 2, or 3. 1 indicates the invoice is sent to the head office, 2 indicates the invoice is sent to the branch office, and 3 indicates the invoice is sent to both offices.

NAME: Bread Discount
FORMAT: Numeric
SIZE: 4 digits
LOCATION IN RECORD: Bytes 9 through 13
DESCRIPTION: The percentage discount customer receives on bread items. The percentage can range from 0 to 99.99%.

```
              NAME:  Confectionary Discount
            FORMAT:  Numeric
              SIZE:  4 digits
LOCATION IN RECORD:  Bytes 14 through 18
       DESCRIPTION:  The percentage discount a customer re-
                     ceives on confectionary items. The
                     percentage can range from 0 to 99.99%.

              NAME:  Invoice Name and Address
            FORMAT:  Character
              SIZE:  100 digits
LOCATION IN RECORD:  Bytes 19 through 119
       DESCRIPTION:  The customer name and address up to 100
                     characters.

              NAME:  Consignee Name and Address
            FORMAT:  Character
              SIZE:  100 digits
LOCATION IN RECORD:  Bytes 120 through 220
       DESCRIPTION:  The consignee's name and address up to
                     100 characters. It may be the same as
                     invoice name.
```

The rest of the fields have been omitted because this is an educational exercise and exact field descriptions are not required.

Example 85

The following series of definitions is another good example. It gives standard data and uses a standard format. It is laid out pictorially, includes a narrative description, and is complete.

INDEX DESCRIPTION

NAME OF INDEX: Stock and Sales Index

CONTAINED IN FILE NAME: Stock and Sales File

FORMAT: Fixed

INDEX TYPE: Tree

LENGTH OF ENTRY: 17 characters

ESTIMATED VOLUME: 2,500 entries

NAME OF FIELDS IN THE ENTRY: STATUS-FLG, STYLE-NUM, LEFT-BRANCH, RIGHT-BRANCH, BUCKET-NUM

LAYOUT OF ENTRY:

STATUS FLAG	STYLE NUMBER	LEFT BRANCH CELL	RIGHT BRANCH CELL	BUCKET NUMBER
1 2	5 6	9 10	13 14	17

FILE DESCRIPTION

NAME OF FILE: Stock and Sales File

REFERENCE NUMBER: C40

TYPE OF LABEL: Standard

ORIGIN OF FILE: External to application

FORMAT: Variable

FILE ORGANIZATION: Indexed

BLOCK LENGTH: Multiples of 512 characters

RECORD LENGTH: Variable

ESTIMATED VOLUME: 2,500 records

NAME OF RECORDS IN THE FILE: Stock and Sales Record

BACKUP/DISPOSITION: Two backup copies of the file will be updated weekly. One tape will be locked in the file library and the other tape will be stored off-site. Reorganization of the file will be performed quarterly. Old backup tapes will be rewritten with "garbage" after the file reorganization has been completed and verified.

9 SYSTEM SPECIFICATION II 177

RECORD DESCRIPTION

NAME OF RECORD: Stock and Sales Record

CONTAINED IN FILE NAME: Stock and Sales File

FORMAT: Variable

IDENTIFIER: Style number

LENGTH OF RECORD: Variable (18,149 characters maximum)

NAME OF FIELDS IN THE RECORD: Highest level subrecord: STYLE-NUM, STYLE-DESC, COMM-RATE, MERCH-GROUP-CODE, SUPPLIER-NUM; Middle level subrecord: SIZE-NUM, SELL-PRICE, PURCH-PRICE, WHOUSE-STOCK, FORW-ORDER; Lowest level sub-record: BRANCH-NUM, SIZE-NUM, BRANCH-ALLOC, BRANCH-STOCK, SALES-QTY

LAYOUT OF RECORD:

HIGHEST LEVEL SUBRECORD:

STYLE NUMBER	STYLE DESCRIPTION	COMMISSION RATE	MERCHANDISING GROUP CODE	SUPPLIER NUMBER
1 5	6 35	36 37	38 39	40 41

MIDDLE LEVEL SUBRECORD:

SIZE NUMBER	SELLING PRICE	PURCHASE PRICE	WAREHOUSE STOCK	FORWARD ORDER MONTH 1	FORWARD ORDER MONTH 2	FORWARD ORDER MONTH 3	FORWARD ORDER MONTH 4	FORWARD ORDER MONTH 5	FORWARD ORDER MONTH 6
1 4	5 8	9 12	13 16	17 20	21 24	25 28	29 32	33 36	37 40

LOWEST LEVEL SUBRECORD:

BRANCH NUMBER	SIZE NUMBER	BRANCH ALLOCATION	BRANCH STOCK	SALES QUANTITY WEEK 1	SALES QUANTITY WEEK 2	SALES QUANTITY WEEK 3	SALES QUANTITY WEEK 4	SALES QUANTITY WEEK 5	SALES QUANTITY WEEK 6
1 2	3 6	7 8	9 10	11 12	13 14	15 16	17 18	19 20	21 22

RECORD DESCRIPTION

NAME OF FIELD: STYLE-NUM (style number)

CONTAINED IN RECORD NAME: Stock and Sales Record—highest level

CONTAINED IN FILE NAME: Stock and Sales File

SIZE OF FIELD: 5 characters

DATE TYPE: numeric

FORMAT: 99999

EDIT REQUIREMENTS: This field must contain a positive integer value that is less than or equal to 99999.

✔ 5. Identify Processing Controls

The system designer must determine the internal and external means of ensuring accuracy, completeness, and authorization of the processed data.

Identify any particular system controls to be used, such as security measures, confidential data, or storage precautions.

Format so information is easy to read and reference.

EXAMPLES FOR SECTION 5: PROCESSING CONTROLS

Example 86

Most of the writing in this example is readable, makes good sense, and gives helpful, well-explained information. However, as the editing shows, some sections can be tightened and reorganized.

9 SYSTEM SPECIFICATION II   179

5. PROCESSING CONTROLS:

Internal Security:

Internal security access will be implemented by the use of operator passwords, hardware dependent terminal identification, and keys to operate terminals. Each terminal will be assigned a physical identification number unique to that particular hardware device. The system will allow that terminal to access approved files and perform specified functions only. For example, terminals at the Board of Voter Registration office will have access to the voter registration file but not the jury selection file. Passwords will also be assigned to individual operators. These passwords will be limited to specific functions, as are terminal identifiers, but will be further limited to use on specific terminals. ~~In summary,~~ For internal security, an individual must have a key to operate a terminal; the terminal must be one that is both authorized for the use of the password and the functions (such as deletion and creation of records) that the operator wishes to perform. ~~Finally,~~ The operator's password must have the clearance to access files and perform desired operations. Terminal passwords will be assigned by the Data Processing Department; operator passwords will also be assigned by the Department after written request from the Board of Voter Registration. ~~System security and the verification of data are~~ The respon-

~~sibility of the~~ Board of Voter Registration. The Data Processing Department *is responsible for system security and verification of data.* will supply the Board with a daily printed report of all changes made to the data base the previous day This report will include operator identification information so that errors can be traced. Verification of the data contained in this report is the responsibility of the Board; changes to correct errors are also made by the Board. Requests for any reports other than daily changes and the 10-day report must be made to the Department as needed. Notification will require a written request on letterhead stationery that includes the signature of at least one Democratic and one Republican member of the Board.

Archival Storage:

Archival storage of the voter registration file is maintained by the Board of Voter Registration in hard copy. [Archival storage of the juror payment file will be maintained by the Data Processing Department on magnetic tape.] *Move to end of paragraph as is, it interrupts the discussion of the voter registration file. Put like ideas together.*

Since changes are made to the voter registration file on a daily basis, the file will have a backup rotation schedule. A backup copy of the file will be made on disk and stored in the department at the end of each business day. A tape copy of the file will be made weekly and stored in the county vault at the Civic Center. Finally, at the end of each month, another tape copy will be made and stored off-site.

Example 87

The standard form of the following example is good. The part labeled "B. FILE BACKUP" is most useful to the operations staff. They can anticipate and plan for the system. The part labeled "C. SECURITY" appears imprecise. See my comments written on the text.

```
                    PROCESSING CONTROLS
     A. SCREEN INPUT VERIFICATION
        1. Verification of screen by input personnel
        2. Verification with normal numeric/character editing
           and range testing where possible (see Field Descrip-
           tions, (p. 5) for details)
     B. FILE BACKUP (STUDENT/CLASS SCHEDULE)
        1. Backup One
           a. When Taken: weekly, all year
           b. Where Stored: Data Processing Department
           c. Duration Stored: one week
        2. Backup Two
           a. When Taken: following close of registration
           b. Where Stored: secure area off-site
           c. Duration Stored: until backup three
        3. Backup Three
           a. When Taken: following mid-semester grading
           b. Where Stored: replaces backup two off-site
           c. Duration Stored: until backup four
        4. Backup Four
           a. When Taken: following end of semester activities
           b. Where Stored: replaces backup three off-site
           c. Duration Stored: until end of following semester
     C. SECURITY
        1. During Registration
           a. Grades: restricted to registrar
           b. Adding or Dropping Classes
              i.  Read/Write: registrar
              ii. Read/Write: counselor
           c. Other Information
              i.  Read Only: counselor
              ii. Read/Write: registrar
        2. After Registration
           a. Student File: Read/Write registrar
           b. Class Schedule File
              i.  Read: college personnel
              ii. Read/Write: dean
```

Handwritten annotations: "Are these the only people who have access? How do they gain access? What prevents others from seeing the information?" "Form looks good but, after analysis, we see it does not provide precise information."

PART THREE   DESIGN

✏ 6. Include Program Narratives

Here the designer records the purpose and major functions of each program. The reader wants to know:

What data are processed
What the input sources will be
What the output documents will be
How algorithms will be processed

EXAMPLES FOR SECTION 6: PROGRAM NARRATIVES

Example 88

The following is a good model. Taken from a student registration and grade handling system, it shows good form, complete information, and has helpful illustrations.

```
Program 2
    A. NAME OF PROGRAM: PRINT CLASS SCHEDULE
    B. PURPOSE OF PROGRAM: To print hard copy of class schedule
       for distribution to faculty and students
    C. INPUT SOURCE OF PROGRAM: Class Schedule File
    D. OUTPUT DOCUMENTS AND FILES OF PROGRAM: Hard copy of
       class schedule (see illustration p. 14a)
    E. PROCESSING ALGORITHM OR PROGRAM:
       Do Until No-more-records
         Read a Record
         Write a Record
       End do
```

```
                         CLASS SCHEDULE
Enter Department Code CS

Dept.      Title  Room  Cr.    Instruct  Prereq.  Time/Day  Max.
No.                     Hr.                                 Enr.
CS 114A    CS     H105  3      Woodall   None     1MWF      70   0
CS 114B    CS     S210  3      Woodall   None     6M        50   0

Press Return for New Department


SAMPLE CLASS SCHEDULE SCREEN
```

Example 89

Examples 89A and 89B illustrate another clear and effective way to present information common to program narratives.

Example 89A

PROGRAM NARRATIVE

NAME OF PROGRAM: Process Movements and Create Movement Checklist

REFERENCE NUMBER: C20

MAJOR FUNCTIONS:
1) Process the eleven types of movements
2) Create the movement checklist
3) Compute control totals and branch cash takings
4) Update stock and sales file and commissions file

INPUT (AND INPUT SOURCE):
1) Punched paper tape from the branches, the warehouse, the sales department, and the purchasing department
2) Stock and sales file
3) Commissions file

OUTPUT (AND OUTPUT SOURCE):
1) Movement checklist (to the branches)
2) Stock and sales file (updated)

3) Commissions file (updated)

4) Control totals and branch cash earnings (retained in memory)

RUN PERIOD: Daily

COMPLEX ALGORITHMS: N/A

Example 89B

PROGRAM NARRATIVE

NAME OF PROGRAM: Produce Suggested Orders List

REFERENCE NUMBER: C22

MAJOR FUNCTIONS: To print a list of probable order quantities

INPUT (AND INPUT SOURCE): Stock and sales file

OUTPUT (AND OUTPUT SOURCE): List containing all information relevant to making decisions regarding supplier order quantities and dates and the suggested orders generated by the computer (to the purchasing department)

RUN PERIOD: Twice weekly

COMPLEX ALGORITHMS: PROCESS FASHION STYLES:

1) Calculate difference between average sales for the first four weeks and the last four weeks of the past six weeks
   a) Rising trend found:
      Largest weekly sales of the six is multiplied by four and deducted from stock and forward orders
   b) Falling trend found:
      Difference is to be subtracted from the lower of the averages and the result multiplied by four
2) Any deficiency printed as suggested order quantity

PROCESS NONFASHION STYLES:

1) Find average weekly sales, multiply by four and deduct from total stock and forward order quantities

2) Any deficiency printed as suggested order quantity

Example 90

Compare this form with the comments that follow.

Program Narrative

DATE ORIGINATED _____
DATE REVISED _____

SYSTEM NAME:
PROGRAM TITLE:
PROGRAM PHASE NAME:
PROGRAMMER:
LANGUAGE:
PURPOSE:

BASIC LOGIC:

FILES:

MESSAGES:

COMMENT
This "narrative" illustrates the need for levels of program design documentation. The description given to the original programmer does not need to be as detailed as that given to the maintenance programmer. The original designer is working on the program at the point the documentation is produced, and understands its logic, sources, etc. But maintenance programmers need details. They will be working on the program at a later point, without consulting the original designer.

A "narrative" such as this addresses both levels. In a clear format, it presents basic information, but goes on to explain material under the headings "Basic Logic," "Purpose," and "Files." A maintenance programmer will not have to search through code looking for this information. Such careful documentation makes a system easy to modify, a good characteristic for any system.

Example 91

The form shown on the next page, another maintenance document, is an excellent cross-reference between programs and files. After any program change, the maintenance programmer knows what files to go to in order to make the change effective for the whole system.

9 SYSTEM SPECIFICATION II

FILE USAGE LIST

SEE ALSO PB
SYSTEM NAME: Out-Patients

FILE NAME(S): OPCHARG

FILE ID: 'OP.PERM.CHARGE'

ORIGINATED: 1-82
BY: JW
REVISED:
BY:

PERMANENT [X]
TEMPORARY [ ]

| INPUT || OUTPUT || I/O (update) ||
JOB STEP	PROGRAM	JOB STEP	PROGRAM	JOB STEP	PROGRAM
OP120140	OPD0140C	OP120150	DRET		
OP120410	OPD0170R	OP132220	DRET		
OP124100	OPD0180R				
OP124120	OPD0190R				
OP124130	OPD0210R				
OP132120	OPBCHRGR				
OP140100	OPD0450R				
OP704100	OPR0010R				
OP140170	OPD0470R				

PART THREE DESIGN

✔ 7. Explain Operating Characteristics

Define major operating characteristics:

> File transactions
> Tape transactions
> Equipment used
> Run time: break into daily, weekly, etc.
> Operating costs: note per run, per month, etc.

Verify information with substantiated figures.

    A system specification is useful to people other than programmers. It helps the operations staff anticipate workloads, equipment, and schedules. Staff members have an opportunity to react and thereby indirectly participate in designing the system. Admittedly, the main responsibility belongs to the designer, but anyone who designs without consulting others is likely to create a mess. Consult others. Let them help you anticipate and prevent problems.

EXAMPLES FOR SECTION 7: OPERATING
CHARACTERISTICS

Example 92

Consider yourself as a part of the operations staff. How helpful is this section to you for scheduling or other planning?

```
                    Operating Characteristics
        A. Files
            1. File 1, File 2: on disk at all times
            2. File 1, File 2: backups at specified times (see p. 11)
        B. Tapes: four for backup and turnaround
        C. Equipment Used:
            1. Available
                a. one Hewlett-Packard 3000/series 44
                b. two 3173 disk drives (50 megabytes each)
                c. one Hewlett-Packard line printer (800 LPM)
                d. one decollator/burster
                e. sufficient green bar paper (8 ½ × 11 for class
                   list)
                f. sufficient plain paper (8 ½ × 14 for class sche-
                   dule)
                g. one Hewlett-Packard optical character reader
                   (OCR)
```

        2. To be purchased:
            a. preprinted OCR class list forms (8 ½ × 11)
            b. preprinted student grade report forms (4-part carbonless 4 × 8 ½")
            c. blank gummed labels (3 ¹¹⁄₁₆ × 2 ½)
    D. Data Processing Personnel Responsibilities:
        1. Programs 1-8: online continuously
        2. Program 2: print class schedule
            a. Burst and collate one copy of class schedule (time: 20 minutes)
            b. Hand-carry copy to print shop foreman (time: 20 minutes)
        3. Program 5: print faculty class list
            a. Load printer with 8 ½ × 11 green bar paper (time: 5 minutes)
            b. Burst class lists by class (time: 5 minutes, see Appendix C)
            c. Hand carry to registrar (time: 20 minutes)

(The section continues in this way.)

COMMENT

The presentation is not helpful. Things are there to see, but they are buried in the text. For example, the information about "time," "printing," or "hand carrying" will be important to anyone who must anticipate operating this new system, but a person is likely to miss it or must work too hard to find it.

What is the relevance of item "C Equipment Used"? If all that equipment is "Available," what is a person supposed to do with it?

Example 93

In this example both the design and the information are well thought out and functional. The reader easily sees when things happen and who does what.

OPERATING CHARACTERISTICS

The following information is a presentation of the operations cycle of the new stock and sales control system.

TIME PERIOD	FREQUENCY	ACTIVITY	EQUIPMENT USED	RESPONSIBLE EMPLOYEE(S)
8:00 a.m.	daily	receive mailed input		computer operator
8:15 a.m.– 1:00 p.m.	daily	run process to route input data (C20)	tape reader CPU disk unit disks printer	computer operator
8:30 a.m.– 4:30 p.m.	daily	create branch input	cash registers	sales assistants
8:30 a.m.– 4:30 p.m.	daily	create warehouse input	paper tape punches	warehouse keypunch operator
8:30 a.m.– 4:30 p.m.	daily	create sales and purchase department input	paper tape punches	head office keypunch operator
8:30 a.m.– 4:30 p.m.	daily	create input for sales analysis and replenishment listing	standard company forms	sales manager

| 2:00 p.m.–
3:00 p.m. | daily | run pro-
cess to
produce
replen-
ishment
list
(C21) | standard
company
forms
CPU
disk
disk unit | computer
operator |

8. State Restrictions and Trade-offs ✓

If the system's design is affected by certain constraints, say so and explain the effect.

Justify the selection of this system's design. What factors influenced this choice? How does this design satisfy the goals set earlier in the functional specification?

EXAMPLES FOR SECTION 8: RESTRICTIONS AND TRADE-OFFS

Example 94

Practice editing. Mark the text to tighten the writing and to question or correct content.

Constraints and Trade-offs

In evaluating the system we are implementing there are several aspects that should be remembered. These should be reflected upon for continuing evaluation of the system during the implementation. This can assure that everyone involved in the project will understand the basic precepts from which the system evolved.

The primary goal is to save money

A secondary goal is to increase efficiency

We also want to improve the quality of the data

Integrate the voter's registration and jury selection

As we have pointed out in the presentation, there will be a substantial saving as compared with the current procedures. Since the County Auditor and the Courts already budget for their computer terminals the coordination of these systems is a side benefit of the total computerization of local government.

By eliminating duplication of effort and the streamlining of the voter registration functions the proposed system will more than meet the requirement of any user.

By eliminating the addressograph equipment and the "messy" processes associated with this technique the new system will provide increased cost savings in real dollars and in personnel performance. This is most evident with the operators of the addressograph who will no longer need to "dress down" when operating the printing functions. In fact, the operations will be completely controlled viz the computer terminals located within the user's office.

As you can read, we feel that this system will improve your daily activities on all fronts. There are however some aspects of the system which must be configured around the state and

9 SYSTEM SPECIFICATION II

local guidelines for each office involved. Let me now draw your attention to some of these, they are:

    Signature documents in voter's registration

    Duplicate sets of listing for all political parties

    Hardcopy of entire file

    Signature of Judge on Jury payments form

REWRITE
Compare your editing with mine.

Constraints & Trade-offs:

In evaluating the system we are implementing ~~there are~~ several aspects ~~that should be~~ to remembered. ~~These should be reflected upon for continuing evaluation of the system during the implementation. This can assure~~ so that everyone involved in the project will understand the basic ~~precepts from which the system evolved.~~ objects of the system are as follows:

make structure alike and identify third and fourth goal

1. The primary goal is (to save money)

Is this another part of goal 2 or a third goal?

2. A secondary goal is (to increase efficiency) ?

3. ~~We also want~~ a third goal is (to improve the quality of the data)

4. a fourth goal is ~~to~~ Integrate the voter's registration and jury selection

First three are sentences. The fourth is a fragment. Make all alike.

It is not clear whether this is a comment on goal 1 or something new.

~~As we have pointed out in the presentation~~ There will be a substantial saving as compared with the current procedures. Since, the County Auditor and the Courts already budget for their computer terminals, the coordination of these systems is a [Seems out of place. Should "to coordinate" to goal 5?] side benefit of the total computerization of local government.

[Is this a comment on goal 2?] By eliminating duplication of effort and ~~the~~ *by* streamlining of the voter registration functions, the proposed system will ~~more than~~ meet the requirements of any user.

[Is this a comment on goal 1, goal 3?] By eliminating the addressograph equipment and the "messy" processes associated with this technique, the new system will provide increased cost savings in real dollars and in personnel performance. This is most evident with the operators of the addressograph, who will no longer need to "dress down" when [what does this mean? what does "dressing down" have to do with cost savings and performance?] operating the printing functions. In fact, the operations will [If these are comments where is the comment on goal 4?] be completely controlled via the computer terminals located within the user's office.

~~As you can read, we feel that~~ This system will improve your daily activities. ~~on all fronts.~~ There are, however, some aspects of the system which must be configured around the state and local guidelines for each office involved. ~~Let me now draw your attention to~~ Some of these, ~~they~~ are ~~the following~~:

Signature documents in voter's registration

Duplicate sets of listing for all political parties [What is the point of saying this? How does it relate to objectives of the system?]

Hardcopy of entire file

Signature of Judge on Jury payments form

Example 95

This example clearly shows the alternative considered, the choice made, and the reason for that choice. It anticipates questions a client or another analyst might have. It is direct and to the point.

TRADE-OFFS

	CONSIDERATION	CHOICE	BENEFIT
1.	Adding more memory to card computer	Develop new system	Processing time reduced, no card files
2.	Mainframe computer	Minicomputer	More adaptable to situation, mainframe too large
3.	Microcomputer	Minicomputer	More adaptable to situation, micro too small
4.	Sequential of direct files	Index-sequential files	Faster and easier access
5.	Online or batch environment	Online	Faster updating of files
6.	Write or purchase sort/merge package	Purchase	Cheaper for customer, very adaptable to language
7.	Write or purchase auditing package	Purchase	Cheaper for customer, easy installation into operating system
8.	Write or purchase system software	Write	Cheaper for customer, little, if any, initial maintenance
9.	300 line/min printer	600 line/min printer	Doubled speed of printing times
10.	Manual forecast	Automated forecast	Better accuracy, much quicker

Example 96

This is another example that effectively presents alternatives and benefits. Using paragraphs and complete sentences formalizes the presentation, but the heading and numbered list help to make the information easy to read and understand.

TRADE-OFFS

Two alternative methods for solving ABC's problems were considered before a final decision was made.

Alternative 1:
The first method was a semimanual system requiring key-operated machines. This method would require additional staff and was likely to cause confusion and errors. Therefore, it was not chosen.

Alternative 2:
The second method was the employment of punched cards and the associated machines such as sorters, tabulators, and an electronic calculator. The punched card machines were quickly becoming obsolete and were not suitable for the other data processing applications at ABC. Because of these problems, this method was not regarded as a real solution either.

Adopted Method:
The adopted method was the utilization of a computer on a service bureau basis. The intense competition between service bureaus made the method the most economical. Magnetic tape was determined to be the most suitable for the file storage. The decision was based on:

1. A direct access file would be straightforward requiring little operator involvement. When considering the relatively complex interrelationships of the item specification files, this is important.
2. The service bureau rental charge for magnetic tape reels to store the needed files during their creation and afterwards was the least expensive.
3. The file organization would be less complicated when making amendments to the cost file, especially those associated with the insertion and deletion of lower level items into those higher levels.

The problem's complexity and the lack of data processing experience of ABC's staff resulted in the choice of a service bureau. The computer used will be equipped with magnetic tape and capable of accepting paper tape as its input.

9. Show Costs and Schedules ✔

Any project should be brought in on cost and on time. In order to do so, cost and schedules must be projected so that managers can budget and plan.

The following information is helpful:
  Costs:
    Development and installation costs
    Special equipment or upgrade costs
    Data conversion costs
    Training costs
  Scheduling:
    Project milestone dates

EXAMPLES FOR SECTION 9: COSTS AND SCHEDULES

Example 97

How helpful is this cost statement for budgeting? What improvements do you suggest?

COST/BENEFIT ESTIMATES

I. Estimated MIS Development Costs:

	DIRECT	INDIRECT	TOTAL
Study (40 hrs. @ $24/hr.)	$0	$ 960	$ 960
Design (80 hrs. @ $24/hr.)	0	1,920	1,920
Programming (160 hrs. @ $45/hr.)	0	7,200	7,200
Computer Testing (12 hrs. @ $45/hr.)	0	540	540
TOTAL	$0	$10,620	$10,620

II. Estimated Annual Production Costs:

Computer Time (5 hrs./yr. @ $45/hr.) $ 0 $ 225 $ 225

III. Estimated Annual Savings or Contributions to Profits:

```
Data Control (520 hrs. @ $14/hr.) =   $7,280
Data Services (50 hrs. @ $15/hr.) =      750
                                      _____
     TOTAL ANNUAL SAVINGS              $8,030
```

COMMENT
The format is well organized and well presented. The breakdown of costs by hours and costs-per-hour is good.

My question is whether the financial staff will accept and understand the basis for these figures. Does the writer need to justify the costs?

Example 98

The costs section of the following example is well designed. Information is partitioned. Figures are easy to see. Group totals and a grand total are given. The question is whether the information is useful. For example, does the reader of "Training Costs" need to know the destination of the "travel" and what course the "materials" are for? Is the information precise enough to be accepted?

The schedule section is useless. The design does not let the reader know dates or if weeks overlap.

```
                        COSTS AND SCHEDULES
Costs
   Software development costs:
      Senior analyst                      1×_____  =  _____
      System programmer/analyst           1×_____  =  _____
      Programmer/analyst                  1×_____  =  _____

                       Total                           ======
   Installation costs:
      Cash registers                     70×_____  =  _____
      Paper tape punches                  2×_____  =  _____
      Paper tape reader                   1×_____  =  _____
      Exchangeable disk storage unit      1×_____  =  _____
      Furniture                            ×_____  =  _____

                       Total                           ======
```

```
Equipment costs:
    Cash registers                          70×_____ = _____
    Paper tape punches                       2×_____ = _____
    Paper tape reader                        1×_____ = _____
    Exchangeable disk storage unit           1×_____ = _____
    Disks                                    2×_____ = _____

                    Total                                _____

Personnel costs:
    Keypunch operators                       2×_____ = _____

                    Total                                _____

Training costs:
    Travel expenses                         70×_____ = _____
    Course materials                        70×_____ = _____

                    Total                                _____

Conversion costs:
    Senior analyst                           1×_____ = _____
    System programmer/analyst                1×_____ = _____
    Programmer/analyst                       1×_____ = _____
    Testing team                              ×_____ = _____

                    Total                                _____

                  Grand Total                            _____

Schedule
    System definition                        _____ weeks
    Software design                          _____ weeks
    Software development                     _____ weeks
    Software system testing                  _____ weeks
    System acceptance testing                _____ weeks
```

Example 99

The Schedule Plan on the next page communicates poorly. Decide why.

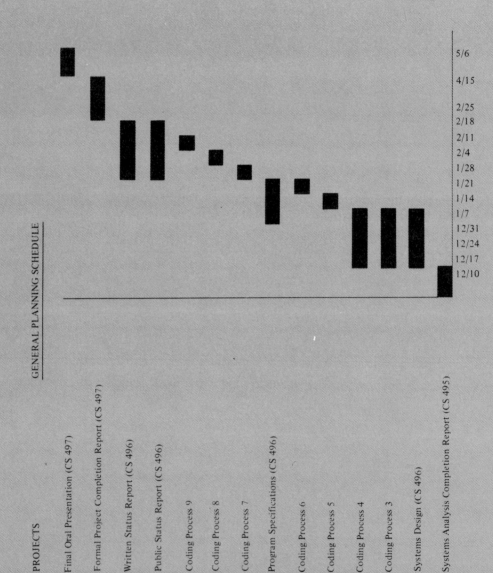

COMMENT
This schedule is impossible: it is difficult to follow across from the project to the block that corresponds to it; it is hard to follow up from dates through the blocks in order to determine time; it is also irritating to have the dates printed in one direction and the blocks in another.

The document's design is poor, and the information is presented ineffectively. The schedule should be lined so the reader can make correspondences between projects and blocks of time.

The title should name the specific project. The name of the person who designed the schedule and the date it was designed also should appear on this page.

Example 100

This plan is useless. Decide why.

Implementation Scheduling Plan

Most tasks for the implementation of the proposed system can be done consecutively after the purchase and installation of the microfiche equipment. It should take approximately 23 days to implement this system. The following bar charts depict the scheduling, in number of days, that will be needed for a successful implementation.

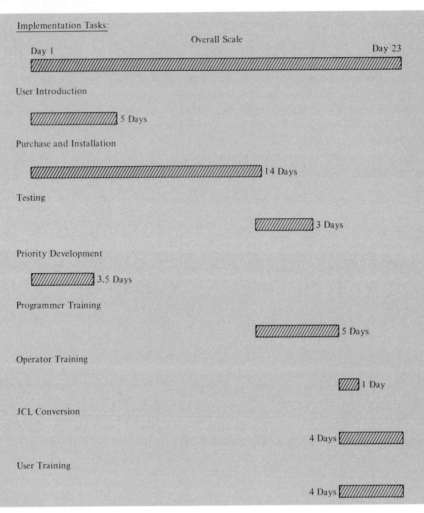

COMMENT

No one can read this. Is the 23-day bar at the top supposed to tell when other activities are done? If so it fails. Look at the "Purchasing and Installation" bar and the "Testing" bar. Are they lined up to mean that testing starts before purchasing and installation are completed? If so, how many days before?

It is possible to begin to read the chart this way: The whole implementation task will take 23 days. It begins with a "user introduction." That takes five days. Next, "purchase and installation" occur. That takes 14 days. Then we "test" for three days. Wait a minute! This is not going to work. There are too many days.

Redesign the chart so the "Overall Scale" is divided into 23 units. Continue those divisions down the page. Line up the activities along the side. Color or mark the bars to show on which of the 23 days each activity will occur. See my rewrite.

Rewrite of Example 100
Implementation Scheduling Plan

Most tasks for the implementation of the proposed system can be done consecutively after the purchase and installation of the microfiche equipment. It should take approximately 23 days to implement this system. The following bar charts depict the scheduling, in number of days, that will be needed for a successful implementation.

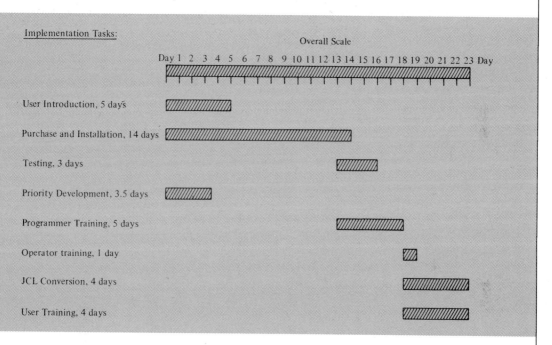

10. Develop a System Test Plan

Will it work? Does it do what it is supposed to do? Everyone wants to know the answers to these questions. To find out, the system must be tested. If errors exist or functions are missing, now is the time to discover and correct them.

Include these objectives when setting up a system test plan:

Set objectives for acceptance.
Schedule the activities that make up the test: Starts when; continues how long; over when?
Determine who will oversee the test and inform that person of procedure and responsibilities.
Inform in advance everyone involved in the test.
Provide instructions to everyone; set procedures.
Establish criteria for acceptance.
Ensure an objective appraisal of performance.

PART THREE DESIGN

General Summary

Look again at a system specification you are writing, have written, or are directing or managing. After considering this chapter, what in your system specification seems like good writing? What needs revising?

CHECKLIST: CHAPTER 9
System Specification II

OUTLINE	
4. DEFINE DATA	Explain the purpose, content, and layout of data.
A. DATA DICTIONARY	A file of all data items, records, and files used within a system.
	Sets accepted meanings.
	Provides language consistency.
	Cross-references data.
	Makes future modifying accurate and complete.
	Design Rules:
	Compile by a system.
	Alphabetize entries.
	Make definitions consistent and accurate.
	Include basic information:
	Data name
	Aliases
	Description
	Format
	Location
	Notes
	The three together complete a file definition.
B. FILES, RECORDS, FIELDS	Construct in a step-down manner.
	Identify the name, purpose, content, and format of each definition.
	Design Rules:
	Explain the purpose of the files and the purpose of the records within the file.
	State why the file design was chosen.
	Picture the information.
	Use a preprinted form or create a standard way of presenting definitions.
	Define by using standard items. See p. 165.
5. IDENTIFY PROCESSING CONTROLS	Determine the internal and external means of ensuring accuracy, completeness, and authorization of the processed data.
	Identify any system controls.
	Format for easy reading and reference.
6. INCLUDE PROGRAM NARRATIVES	Record the purpose and major functions of each program; data processed, input sources, output documents, and processing algorithms.

PART THREE   DESIGN

7.	EXPLAIN OPERATING CHARACTERISTICS	Define major characteristics: file and tape transactions, equipment, run time, and operating costs. Verify information with substantiated figures.
8.	STATE RESTRICTIONS AND TRADE-OFFS	Identify design constraints. Justify the design selection.
9.	SHOW COSTS AND SCHEDULES	Project costs so the project can be on-cost and on-time. Be thorough in the projection. Consider costs such as development, installation equipment, data conversion, personnel, and training. Project milestone dates.
10.	DEVELOP A SYSTEM TEST PLAN	Devise a test to find out if the system works and does what it is supposed to do. Use the objectives on p. 203 to plan a good test.

PART FOUR

IMPLEMENTATION

The ultimate test for any system is whether it can be used efficiently. The analysis may be comprehensive. The design may be beautiful. But if the system cannot be implemented, it is useless.

A system cannot implement itself. It needs people to start, use, and maintain it; but first they must learn how. Providing documentation that teaches how is part of your responsibility as a member of the system development team.

As the system designer or program designer, you could once brainstorm with colleagues who understood you; you could solve technical problems for those who shared your understanding of computers. That in-group luxury is gone. Now your challenge is to communicate your understanding of the system to people who may not know or care about computers, and only want to know what is necessary to perform the job. You designed the system and its programs; you have an obligation to explain the system to others who must maintain or use it.

The work is similar to that of analysis, but with a difference. As an analyst, you communicate with someone who may not understand computers, but that person has an interest in working and talking with you. He or she has requested the system, is responsible for its management, or is paying for it. But when you write for a wider audience of users, not all your readers have the same high level of interest. There is no dialog with the readers; they cannot ask you questions. You are the authority who tells them how to do something. All that you have learned about writing is needed to perform this task.

Manuals teach implementation, and two common documents are the operations manual and the user's manual. The operations manual describes how to set up, operate, solve problems, dismantle, and restart the system. The user's manual teaches how to use the system and its programs.

Both manuals teach how to do things; therefore, authors of both must be able to write effective instructions. I have selected the user's manual to practice our writing and analyzing of instructions because its audience is more diverse. A system may have only a few people qualified to work on its maintenance, but many people with very different qualifications must use its programs. In many cases the manual is the sole means of learning how to do the work or how to correct errors. If the system is in a manufacturing company, bank, or other business that has no data processing department, the user has no local backup when the manual fails to be clear. If office personnel use the system on a shift when no in-house assistance is available and encounter a problem the manual does not solve, they have to wait until help from outside the company arrives or until the regular full shift comes back. Either situation is costly and condemns the manual.

10

User's Manual

What Is a User's Manual and What Is Its Function?

A user's manual is a handbook that instructs the system's user how to operate the hardware, run programs, correct mistakes, and solve typical problems.

Who Writes the Manual and Who Reads It?

The system design team is responsible for writing the system's manuals. Normally, a particular person or a small group will be assigned this task.

The reader is anyone who uses the system. The manual's broad audience includes every level of experience and makes the task difficult.

Determining who your audience is is essential. Do not assume you understand the user. Find out who will use this handbook. What is the user's level of computer literacy?

Work Habits for Writing Good Manuals

PUT YOURSELF IN THE USER'S PLACE

Imagine that you must perform the routine for the first time. Be complete. Tell how to correct errors. Give warnings before problems occur. Tell when the procedure is over. Describe how to sign off or shut down the system.

BE INTERESTED IN THIS WRITING

People in data processing can quickly lose interest in the system once it is designed and programmed. This attitude results in cursory user documentation. Hasty, superficial documentation is foolish because the system will not be used to its potential. It may appear faulty because users have so much trouble running programs, or people may refuse to use it. Any of these conditions hinders the system's success.

PAY PARTICULAR ATTENTION TO FORMAT

Make this document easy to see and refer to. Warnings, comments, and help should be well organized and visible.

USE PICTURES

Show the keyboard, an example of a correct printout, or whatever "picture" will tell users they are operating the system correctly. Think of any technical manual you ever used and liked. Whether it showed you how to put together a child's toy or how to unpack, install, and test your new personal computer, pictures made the instructions clear. Provide the same for your reader.

TEST IT

Test the writing with real users. Revise. Test again.

ORGANIZE AND OUTLINE

Do so to serve the user. What does that person need to know first? Where does the reader need the illustrations placed? Will the user need to use only parts of the manual at a time or as reference? How can you organize so the reader can use the manual in this way?

An outline commonly used is a simple one:

Introduction
Instructions
Index

WRITING SUGGESTIONS

Leave plenty of white space. Separate steps of the procedure from one another.

Tell how long a procedure will take. The user does not want to begin a 50-minute program 10 minutes before lunch. Estimate the time it will take the user to do the task, not how long it would take you.

Give one instruction or one set of instructions at a time.

Format so that you nest instructions that work together.

Separate warnings and comments from instructions. Place them where they will be useful. For example, do not place a warning after instructions for the procedure. Readers do not read ahead.

Create signposts for users at different levels. The experienced user can then skip over elementary information and use the manual more efficiently. Numbers or colors make effective signposts.

Use informative headings, and lots of them.

Tell the reader a picture follows. Do not assume the reader will look ahead and find it.
Tell when and how the procedure is completed.

As usual, we will consider examples. Since the content of any system manual is primarily decided by its designer and its audience, we shall not judge whether the content is either good or bad. Instead we shall judge the presentation.

EXAMPLES FOR WRITING A USER'S MANUAL

Example 101

Parts of two examples of a user's manual for a peripheral data processor (P.D.P.) follow. Compare and evaluate the individual parts. Both manuals are for a group of university students with no knowledge or experience with word processors. All references are to specific facilities of the particular university.

Cover Page, Manual A

The cover sheet is a blank page.

Cover Page, Manual B

```
            PERIPHERAL DATA PROCESSOR
                    (P.D.P.-11)
                WORD PROCESSING MANUAL



              Date: February 8, 1983




                          by
                      Jack Sprat
                    Raymond Poliakoff
                     Lucile Round
                      Ted Stone
```

PART FOUR   IMPLEMENTATION

COMMENT
A title page formalizes the manual. Manual A should have one. Manual B's title page tells what the manual is about, when it was prepared, and who prepared it. All this information is relevant. The date lets one know how recent the manual is; the authors let one know whom to contact if questions arise.

Suggestions for Improving Manual B

More information would make this title page more useful. Who is the audience? The personnel of a company? The general public?
 Who are the people listed? Give their titles. Whom do they work for?
The "by" appears awkward. Is it needed?

Table of Contents, Manual A

```
                    TABLE OF CONTENTS


     INTRODUCTION                                 3
     HOW TO LOG ON                                4
     USING UEDIT                                  5
     USING RUNOFF                                 8
     HOW TO LOG OFF                              13
```

Table of Contents, Manual B

```
                    TABLE OF CONTENTS


     INTRODUCTION                                 1
     LOGON PROCEDURE                              4
     UEDIT PROCEDURE                              6
     RUNOFF                                       8
        INTRODUCTION                              8
        FORMAT                                    9
        COMMANDS                                 11
        RUNNING RUNOFF                           18
     LOGOFF PROCEDURE                            19
     EXAMPLE                                     20
```

COMMENT
I prefer Manual B. The spacing is more pleasing. The breakdown of material under "RUNOFF" seems helpful.

Introduction, Manual A

This document is to show a beginner the basic steps in logging on to the P.D.P.-11/34, creating a document (usually a program) to be edited, using RUNOFF commands and submitting the program to be printed out either on the terminal you are working on or a printer.

The steps in the process will be the following:

1. Define the LOGON process
2. Define how to use UEDIT
3. Define how to get out of UEDIT
4. Define how to run RUNOFF
5. Define the commands available in RUNOFF
6. Define how to LOGOFF

COMMENT

Breaking the process into six steps and listing them is effective. The first sentence is poorly written. See the edited version for a better way.

Rewrite

This manual shows a user (1) the basic steps in logging on to the P.D.P.-11/34; (2) how to create a program for editing; (3) how to use RUNOFF commands and submit the program either displayed on the terminal or printed out on a printer.

Introduction, Manual B

Consider this introduction by paragraphs. Think of yourself as a user. How do you react? Compare your reactions to mine.

Welcome to the world of word processing. This manual guides and instructs the beginner in word processing—text processing of narrative records that can be entered, stored, retrieved, and changed.

To use this guide, you need no special skills, but if you type that is helpful.

COMMENT

Good points

    The tone because it is conversational and willing to inform.
    The writer's defining "word processing"—"text processing . . ."
    The statement of qualifications for using the guide—"To use this guide . . ."

First, let me introduce you to the Peripheral Data Processor, or P.D.P.-11, the computer you will work with. In this work world, you are the master and the P.D.P. is your slave. You give instructions and the P.D.P. carries them out. You will use the P.D.P. as a word processor, which means that you will type text into the computer and be able instantaneously to edit that text. The computer can then display or print the revised, error-free text. Obviously, this process can be very useful to you as a student because you will not have to retype assignments in order to correct them.

COMMENT
The analogy of the P.D.P. as "slave" gives color to the text and lightens the tone.

This manual takes you step by step through the use of the word processing system on the P.D.P.-11. To begin you must obtain a password from the director of the P.D.P.-11 or the person in charge of the P.D.P. room, Room 117 in the Engineering and Science Building. This password allows you to use the computer. You will be instructed in its usage in the LOGON section on page 4 of this manual. After obtaining a password, go to Room 117 (E/S Building) where the P.D.P. is located. Along the right wall, you will see several keyboards with television-like screens attached. These are what we call the "terminals" or "monitors" and are used to type and display the text. You will do your word processing here. Sit down at an available terminal and examine the keyboard. Note that it resembles a standard typewriter. However, there are several keys that are different, and they will be explained later when you are instructed to use them. The terminal does not physically type on paper; as you hit the keys, you will see an image of what you are typing on the screen. On a typewriter, the carriage position indicates where you are typing on the paper, but on the terminal you will see a small white box, called the "cursor," that shows where the next character will appear if you type anything on the keyboard. The cursor control keys (to be explained later) guide the cursor around the screen in a left-right-up-down fashion.

COMMENT
The simple, detailed information is excellent for this user. However the paragraph form makes it difficult to read and refer to. I suggest revising with an opening statement followed by a list of instructions.

Rewrite
This manual takes you step by step through the use of the word processing system on the P.D.P.-11:

1. Obtain a password from . . .

2. Go to Room 117 in the . . .

3. Notice along the right wall several keyboards . . .

4. Sit down at an available terminal . . .

   You are now ready to begin your lesson in word processing. Follow this manual step by step. If you have questions, contact the person in charge of the P.D.P. room.

COMMENT
The conclusion continues the conversational tone that is appropriate for this audience.
   Telling whom to contact if there is trouble is a good idea.

Illustration, Manual A
No illustration

Illustration, Manual B

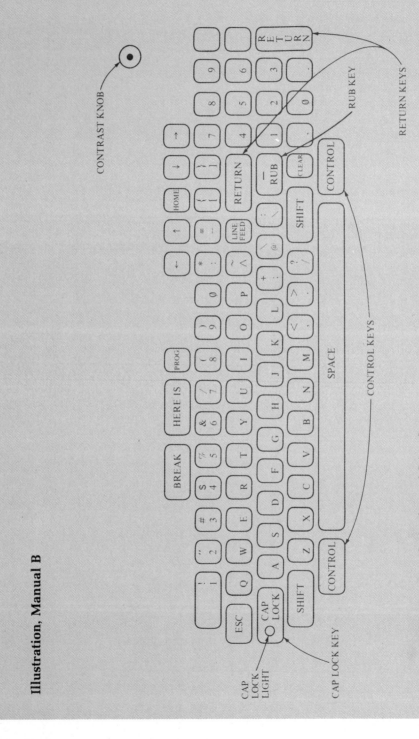

P.D.P.-11 Terminal Keyboard Display

COMMENT

The picture is helpful for this audience of students. As they take the manual home to study, they can use the picture of the keyboard to imagine a procedure more accurately. Without it, the user must remember what the keyboard at school looks like.

Suggestion for Improvement

Include the illustration as an item in the table of contents.

Example 102

The next two examples present the LOGON procedure from the two P.D.P. manuals studied in Example 101.

    Review the "Writing Suggestions" for manuals (pp. 210–212) and decide why Manual A is a poor model for writing instructions.

Manual A

```
                    The LOGON Procedure
Before you can go any further you must ask the system manager for
a password and code number. The current system manager is Mr.
Somebody, and he can be found in the Engineering Science Build-
ing, in room 117A. The P.D.P.-11/34 (the computer we will be
working with) is also located in room 117, and anyone who is
currently enrolled at the university is eligible to use the
computer.

LOGGING ON the computer is jargon for gaining access to the
computer files. To get on this computer perform the following:
   Step 1. Type in "hello" and hit the return key.
   Step 2. The computer is now asking for your code number that
   you received from the computer staff. This number will
   actually consist of two numbers separated by a comma. Please
   type these now and hit the return key.
   Step 3. The computer will now ask for your password. What you
   type next will not appear on the screen; this is normal. You
   now need to type in the password that was given to you by the
   computer staff when you got your code number and hit the re-
   turn key.
If you made a mistake somewhere along the way you will have to
begin again at the step where you entered your code number. If
you have successfully logged on the computer, you will see the
word "ready" appear on your screen in a few minutes.
```

PART FOUR IMPLEMENTATION

COMMENT
1. More than one instruction is given at a time.
2. The instructions are hard to read. For example, in step 2, the command "Please type these now..." is at the end of the paragraph. The command is buried under comments that precede it.
3. Giving instructions in paragraphs is poor form. It makes the information hard to read and to use.
4. Comments and instructions are mixed. They should be separated.
5. The information that begins "If you made a mistake" comes too late. The user may not read that far; instead he or she may just give up.
6. The introductory comments under "Before you go any further" do not belong in this set of instructions under "LOGON." The user does not want to get all ready to do the "Logon Procedure" and then find out he or she has to get a password and code number.

Manual B. This sample of the same procedure is more effective. See the comments.

LOGON PROCEDURE

Notes:
The following shaded keyboard keys will be used:

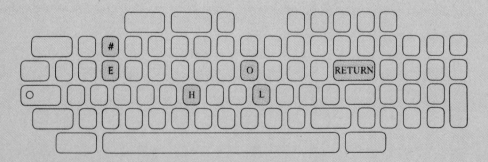

(return) means hit the return key.
<u>CAPITAL</u> letters underlined are letters or numbers you type in.
CAPITAL letters not underlined are messages that appear on the screen.
STEP 1: Type HELLO (return)
       If the terminal replies
           PLEASE SAY HELLO
           BYE
       then repeat STEP 1.

> If the terminal replies with a message like the following:
>   RSTS V7.0-07 UNIV OF E'VILLE JOB nn KB nn
>   DD/MM/YY (date) NN:NN (current time)
>   #
> go to Step 2.
>
> If the terminal replies
>   RSTS/E IS OFF THE AIR
>   ? NO LOGINS
> the computer is busy and you should return in 15 minutes.
>
> Step 2. Your cursor will now be beside the # sign. Type your account number in the form:
>   NN,NN (return).
> The terminal should reply
>   PASSWORD
> If so, go to STEP 3, else repeat STEP 2.
>
> If after four tries, the word PASSWORD does not appear, you will be automatically logged off, and you will need to return to the person who assigned you your password and have it corrected.
>
> Step 3. The cursor will now be beside PASSWORD. Type your <u>PASSWORD</u> (return). The password will not appear on the screen.
>
> If the terminal replies
>   INVALID ACCESS ENTRY ACCESS DENIED
> return to STEP 2.
>
> If the terminal replies
>   WELCOME TO THE UNIVERSITY
>   RSTS/E TIME-SHARING (possibly a message after this)
>   READY
> you are now logged on and ready for the UEDIT procedure.

COMMENT

Picturing the keys to be used in this procedure is a good idea. The format and spacing are good and consistent. The directions are accurate and full.

  Common problems/mistakes are identified and the user is instructed what to do if they occur.

Suggestion for Improvement

Format so that commands to the user are separate from author's comments or explanations.

PART FOUR IMPLEMENTATION

Example 103

A manual needs to conclude—to tell the user she or he is finished. Consider the following example from Manual B which effectively instructs the user how to logoff and politely bids the user goodby ("Good morning . . .).

Manual B

LOGOFF PROCEDURES

Notes:
The following shaded keyboard keys will be used.

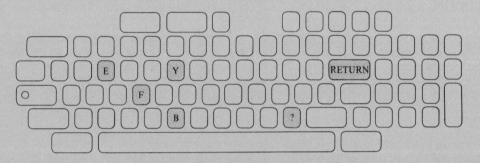

(return) means hit the return key
CAPITAL letters underlined are letters or numbers you type in.
CAPITAL letters not underlined are messages that appear on the screen.

Step 1. Type BYE (return).
   If the terminal replies
      ?WHAT?
      READY
   then repeat STEP 1.

   If the terminal replies
      ENTER '?' FOR HELP.
      CONFIRM:
   You now have three choices:
   1. You can type F which stands for Fast Log off and will give you the message:
      LOGGED OFF
      Choose this option when there are no statistics.
   2. You can type ? which gives you a listing of commands to use to Log off.
      Choose this option when you are uncertain what procedure to use. HELP will appear on the screen.

3. You can type <u>Y</u> which gives your run time and connect time like the following:
   ```
   SAVED ALL FILES
   SU; IS EMPTY
   DL2; HAS NO STORAGE ALLOCATED
   JOB # USER nn,nn LOGGED OFF KBH: AT (current time)
   DD/MM/YY
   SYSTEM RSTS V7.007 UNIV
   RUNTIME WAS nn.n SECONDS
   CONNECT TIME WAS n MINUTES,n SECONDS
   ```
   Choose this option when you use statistics.
GOOD MORNING (AFTERNOON OR EVENING)

Example 104

Manual B (see Examples 101 to 103) closes by including the following two examples of text. These become good references. The user can compare them to his or her own work. My question is whether these examples should be earlier in the manual—perhaps after the keyboard illustration in the Introduction. The user would know they exist, perhaps use them more, and have an idea how the text will look on the screen and after it is printed.

The first figure shows how the text looks on the screen before it is processed by the computer. The second figure shows the text after it is printed.

Figure 1

```
.LH 10
.RM 75
&M &E &M &O &R &A &N &D &U &M
.S 2
TO:   DR. ANN STUART
.S
FROM:   NANCY HAGAN
.I 7
KIM FOSTER
.I 7
JAYNE LORD
.I 7
DIANA KROEGER
.I 7
```

```
            CHRIS TAYLOR
            .I 7
            AARON WILHELM
            .I 7
            CATHY MAIDLOW
            .S
            DATE:   FEBRUARY 8, 1983
            .S
            SUBJECT:   MANUAL ON HOW TO USE WORD PROCESSING ON P.D.P.-11
            .I 10
                    INTERFACING WITH UEDIT, AND RUNOFF.
            .S 3
            .P
            WORD PROCESSING CAN BE MADE EASY WITH THE USE OF RUNOFF, UEDIT,
            AND, OF COURSE, THE P.D.P.-11. THIS MANUAL TEACHES HOW TO USE A
            WORD PROCESSING PROGRAM AND EMPHASIZES THE BENEFITS:
            .S 2
            .I 4
            1.   MISTAKES CAN EASILY BE CORRECTED.
            .S
            .I 4
            2.   MULTIPLE COPIES CAN BE MADE.
            .S 2
            .I 4
            3.   SUBSTITUTION OF PARAMETERS IS EASY.
            .S 2
            .P
            LET US KNOW IF YOU WOULD LIKE ADDITIONAL COPIES OF THIS MANUAL TO
            DISTRIBUTE THROUGHOUT YOUR CLASSES. WE ARE POSITIVE YOUR STU-
            DENTS WILL APPRECIATE THIS.
            .P
            WE CAN BE CONTACTED AT:
            .S 2
            .I 30
            WORDPRO INC. CO.
            .S
            .I 30
            C/O DEPARTMENT 03
            .S
            .I 30
            P.O. BOX 2913
            .S
            .I 30
            EVANSVILLE IN 47714
```

Figure 2

```
                    MEMORANDUM

TO:    DR. ANN STUART
FROM:  NANCY HAGAN
       KIM FOSTER
       JAYNE LORD
       DIANA KROEGER
       CHRIS TAYLOR
       AARON WILHELM
       CATHY MAIDLOW

DATE:    FEBRUARY 8, 1983

SUBJECT:   MANUAL ON HOW TO USE WORD PROCESSING ON P.D.P.-11
           INTERFACING WITH UEDIT, AND RUNOFF.
```

WORD PROCESSING CAN BE MADE EASY WITH THE USE OF RUNOFF, UEDIT, AND OF COURSE, THE P.D.P.-11. THIS MANUAL TEACHES HOW TO USE A WORD PROCESSING PROGRAM AND EMPHASIZES THE BENEFITS:

1. MISTAKES CAN EASILY BE CORRECTED.

2. MULTIPLE COPIES CAN BE MADE.

3. SUBSTITUTION OF PARAMETERS IS EASY.

LET US KNOW IF YOU WOULD LIKE ADDITIONAL COPIES OF THIS MANUAL TO DISTRIBUTE THROUGHOUT YOUR CLASSES. WE ARE POSITIVE YOUR STUDENTS WILL APPRECIATE THIS.

WE CAN BE CONTACTED AT:

                        WORDPRO INC. CO.

                        C/O DEPARTMENT 03

                        P.O. BOX 2913

                        EVANSVILLE IN 47714

Example 105

This system is designed for an independent pharmacy. No one in the drugstore has computer training; therefore this manual must instruct the personnel to perform the work and to solve common problems. Otherwise, outside help must be called, and that is both time consuming and costly.

Decide how effective this manual is and compare your opinion with my comments within the text.

USER'S MANUAL FOR PHARMACY INFORMATION SYSTEM

This system was designed with an inexperienced user in mind. All required user inputs are prompted by the computer. Procedures are menu driven with several options from which the user chooses. Some general features about the system are presented below:

1. Inverse Mode (black and white) messages are generally prompts for user input or error messages. Error messages are preceded by a bell.
2. Some prompt messages are in normal mode; Be sure you read the messages to see if some input is required.
3. Always press "return" after an input.
4. Some inputs have specific length requirements. If a user's input is out-of-bounds for length, a bell will sound and a message will be printed telling the user what correction to make and asking for another input.
5. Some inputs are optional and the data can be excluded by just pressing "return." Others are required and an entry of just "return" will result in an error message and another request for the data.
6. Some procedures take awhile; please be patient.

COMMENT

Look at the first three sentences of the introductory paragraph. Do the second and third sentences relate to the first sentence? In other words, are the "inputs" prompted and the procedures "menu driven" because inexperienced people will be using this system? The relationship of ideas is not clear.

If the user is "inexperienced," how is that person going to understand language like "inputs are prompted by the computer," and "procedures are menu driven"?

I do not understand some things listed in the "general features:"

Item 1: What does "generally" mean? What are the messages other times? What does "bell" mean? How loud is it? I may be embarrassed. Does this mean that "in addition to the prompt," error messages are preceded by a bell?

Item 2: What distinguishes "normal mode"?
Item 5: How do I know what is "optional" and what is "required"?
Item 6: What does "awhile" mean? How long should I wait?

Procedure 1: SYSTEM START-UP

To get started, you must load the system from the disk and run it as follows. This must be done each time the computer is turned on.

1. Turn on the computer and the monitor.
2. Wait for the] symbol to appear.
3. Type LOAD DSTUAR and press return.
4. Wait until the red light on the disk drive goes off and the] reappears with the flashing cursor. It will take 45-90 seconds.
5. Type RUN.
6. Enter the date when it is asked for (press return).
7. The menu will appear like this:
   1. create new files
   2. add to an existing file
   3. retrieve a record from a file
   4. change or delete a record
   5. process a prescription
   6. produce an insurance form
   7. update a file
   8. exit

Select your activity by entering the correct number followed by "return." Each activity is described in the following procedures. When the activity is finished, the system will return to the master menu.

If an error occurs or the] and flashing cursor appears, you can restart the system by starting at step 2 above.

COMMENT

Introductory Comments: How do I "load" the system from the "disk"? Are the seven steps a procedure for loading the system? It is not clear.

  Item 1: How do I "turn on the computer and the monitor"? Are they two separate things?
  Item 4: Where is the "red light"? How is it "on" the disk drive? Does the "flashing cursor" appear also on the disk drive?

Item 5: Do I "press return" after typing RUN? (See 3 and 6.)
Item 6: Why is press return in ( ) in this instruction and not in ( ) in 3?

To avoid repetition and confusion, identify the "menu" items by a, b, c, not 1, 2, 3.

Why is the information after the menu items in paragraph form? Why not make it number 8? The writer is still giving instructions, "Select your activity. . . ."

The "error" message is ineffective. It comes too late. It is too hard to find.

SUMMARY COMMENT

This manual tries to say things simply and to format effectively. It looks clean and readable. Yet it does not effectively serve the "inexperienced user." Too many questions come up. Too many instructions are incomplete or ambiguous. No pictures exist for the user to use in order to *compare* his or her work to correct work.

Example 106

Instructions are the essence of a user's manual. While no one way is the best way to write them, the following example illustrates basic writing rules. Assume the user understands language like "disk pack" and "scratch tape." Look at the format and determine its errors.

```
                  Operation Instruction for A101
This job stream is used to select married alumni from the Alumni
File.

    1. Mount the REMOVE4 disk pack on disk drive 200.
    2. Mount a large scratch tape on tape drive 181.
    3. Run the A101 job deck into the reader.
    4. When the console asks for the date, type the current date
       in the following format:
           //DATE,05/05/81
    5. After the job has ended, BG WAITING FOR WORK will be dis-
       played on the console. Remove the scratch tape and the
       REMOVE4 disk pack.
    6. Print the output on fanfold paper. Lay the printout and job
       deck on the output table.

       If the job cancels type in MSG BG and have the system pro-
       grammer look at why it cancelled.
```

COMMENT
Simple errors hinder the instructions' effectiveness.

1. Items 4 and 5 begin with phrases ("When the console," "After the job"). Others begin with verbs ("Mount," "Print"). All instructions should be alike.
2. The format for the date is not precise. The first "05" could mean day or month.
3. Two instructions are given in item 6—"print" and "lay." The other items contain only one. The user will not expect two and therefore may not see the second one.
4. The "If the job cancels" comment is poorly placed. Warnings or comments need to be close to what they relate to.

Rewrite. The errors are corrected.

Operating Instructions for A101

This job stream is used to select married alumni from the Alumni File.

1. Mount the REMOVE4 disk pack on disk drive 200.
2. Mount a large scratch tape on tape drive 181.
3. Run the A101 job deck into the reader.   <u>Comment:</u> If the job cancels, type in MSG BG and have the system programmer look at why it cancelled.
4. Type the current date in the following form when the console asks for the date:
    //DATE, 12/29/81
5. Wait for the comment
    BG WAITING FOR WORK
6. Remove the scratch tape and the REMOVE4 disk pack.
7. Print the output on fanfold paper.
8. Lay the printout and job deck on the output table.

COMMENT
The format is now consistent, the instructions are written alike; one instruction is given for each number; the comment is placed where it is helpful; and the ambiguity of the date is cleared up.

Example 107

The following excerpts from two different manuals illustrate the effectiveness of writing instructions in a simple, clear, and complete way. Use these as models or let them suggest other ways for you to write so that the user can perform his or her work correctly.

Example 107A

BROWN CITY BANK

Trust Department's User's Manual for Part Time Computer Clerk

PART ONE

Hi! I am your friendly user's manual. I am to be used for the purpose of training you, the part-time computer clerk in the Trust Department at Brown City Bank.

In this manual you will learn how to run the first two jobs on your list of things to do each night. Each job has a specified procedure associated with it that you are to follow. Each procedure is broken down into steps (instructions) with a picture of how the screen will look following each step.

The format for each instruction will usually be one or two simple statements with anything that you are to enter into the computer in capital letters. You will be keypunching on a computer terminal, such as the one pictured below.

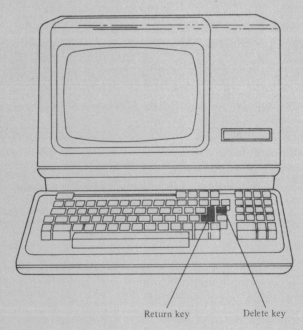

Return key   Delete key

As you can see, it consists of a TV-like screen and a keyboard much like a standard office typewriter. There are two keys, however, that are important to recognize. They are labeled in the picture above. The first is the return key. Press this key after each instruction you keypunch. This key actually causes the instruction to be sent to the computer. The second important key is the delete key, which is much like the backspace key on a regular typewriter. Press this key and the last character keypunched will be erased.

Each time a picture of the screen is shown, anything on the screen that you will have keypunched will be circled. The two jobs you will learn to run are:
 1. Trust Master LOG Report (TMLOGR)
 2. Trial Balance

You need not worry what each of these reports does or means, because your job does not require the understanding of the reports you will be running. So, all you need to do is follow simple instructions and you will do just fine.

TMLOGR

1. A blank screen with a prompt (>) will be on the screen when you first sit down at the terminal.

```
     >
```

2. Type HELLO. Hit the return key.

```
     >HELLO
```

PART FOUR   IMPLEMENTATION

3. The words "User:" and "Password:" will appear. Type 1,8 following "User:". Hit the return key. Type LGT following "Password:". Hit the return key.

```
>HELLO

User: 1,8

Password: LGT
```

4. A prompt will appear on the screen. Type RUN TSK:TMLSTP. Hit the return key. Type PIP TM????.DDF/L. Hit the return key.

```
>HELLO

User: 1,8

Password: LGT

>RUN TSK:TMLSTP

>PIP TM????.DDF/L
```

Example 107B

SECTION I
LOG-ON INSTRUCTIONS

1.0 Log-on

1.1 Begin the log-on procedure by turning the terminal on. The ON-OFF switch is located in the bottom right-hand corner of the terminal. Push the switch up until it clicks. After the terminal is turned on the CURSOR will appear in the top left corner of the screen.

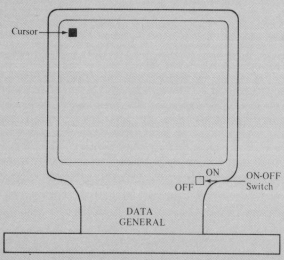

NOTE: If the response to any action is not as described, STOP, and notify the computer manager immediately.

1.2 Log-on continues by pressing the ENTER key.

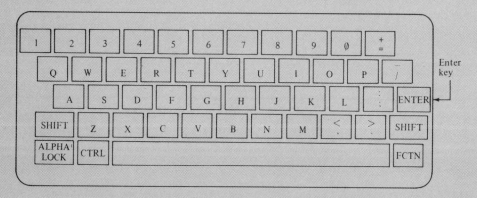

The computer system will respond with the following display on the screen.

```
AOS DATA GENERAL
DATE XX/XX/XX TIME XX.XX.XX
USERNAME:
```

1.3   Type the valid username which is EXPLOSIVE and press the ENTER key to signal to the computer that you are ready for the next step.

1.4   After the username has been entered, the following display will appear on the screen.

```
PASSWORD
```

Type in a valid password and press the ENTER key.
NOTE: The password will not be displayed on the screen as it is typed in. This is for security purposes.

1.5   The computer system compares the username and password
        pair to see that it is valid. If it is not, the screen will
        have the following display.

```
            INVALID USERNAME-
            PASSWORD PAIR.
            USERNAME:
```

General Summary

Review the manuals you are writing or using. How accurate and complete are they? How helpful? How consistent in format and writing style? How easy to reference? How many use illustrations? How clearly is the reader/user identified?

PART FOUR IMPLEMENTATION

CHECKLIST: CHAPTER 10
User's Manual

DEFINITION AND FUNCTION	Provides instructions for the user. Enables the user to operate hardware, run programs, correct mistakes, and solve typical problems.
WRITER	System design team.
AUDIENCE	Anyone who uses the system.
GOOD WORK HABITS	Put yourself in the user's place. Be interested in this writing. Pay attention to format. Test the instructions with real users.
OUTLINE	Introduction Instructions Index
WRITING SUGGESTIONS	Use pictures. Leave plenty of white space. State how long a procedure will take. Give one instruction or set of instructions at a time. Format to nest related instructions. Separate warnings and comments from instructions. Create signposts for users at different levels. Use informative headings, and lots of them. Tell the reader when a picture follows. State when the procedure is completed.

PART FIVE

INFORMAL WRITINGS

The formal documents of a computer system are "public," but a host of informal, private writings appear during the system development cycle. These documents pass between client and members of the system development team and among members of the team itself. Through them, questions are asked, answers given, meetings called, schedules announced, and progress reported.

The fact that working documents are informal and private does not make them unimportant or mean that you can write them carelessly.

We shall study memoranda, status reports, minutes, and summaries.

11

Memoranda, Status Reports, Minutes, Summaries

Memoranda

What the telephone is to conversation, the memorandum is to written communication; it allows us to exchange information informally. Informal does not mean casual. Often information sent by "memo" is crucial; it simply is easier and more appropriate when frequently writing back and forth to use the memorandum rather than to write a formal letter each time.

Some businesses print their own memorandum form on company stationery, others use preprinted forms purchased from business supply houses, still others ask employees to construct the form on blank paper. All are variations of this standard.

```
                        MEMORANDUM
TO:
FROM:
SUBJECT:
DATE:



copies:
attachments:
```

Unfortunately the memorandum does not enjoy a good reputation. People see it as being used excessively, as the primary cause of their desks being buried in paper, as being written when there really is nothing to say, or as the preoccupation of people with trivial minds. Its bad reputation is not the fault of the memorandum itself, but of people who misuse it. If used correctly, the memorandum is an efficient and useful writing form.

SUGGESTIONS FOR WRITING EFFECTIVE MEMORANDA

Write a memorandum only when necessary.
Use a standard form.
Keep to one page if possible.
Organize material so it is easy to see and read: use lists, headings, outlines, and white space.
Type whenever possible; single or double space—be consistent.
Use block or indented style to show paragraphs; be consistent.
Use side heading in full caps or underlined: easy to see, quick to type.
Make headings precise and meaningful.
Identify subsequent pages by subject, date, and page number.
Sign only if you wish; you may initial the memorandum next to your name at the top or at the end of the memorandum.
Omit a complimentary close.
Develop a clean, to-the-point writing style.
Write well:
> Present yourself as well organized, as a logical, no-nonsense, relevant thinker.

EXAMPLES ON MEMORANDA

Example 108

This example is ineffective. Analyze and compare your comments with mine. A rewrite follows.

```
                        MEMORANDUM
                      December 8, 1981



TO:  Dr. John Smith
     Ms. Jane Shaw
     All programming and operations personnel
FROM: Jane Doe
SUBJECT: S222P
```

COMMENT
Place the date in the conventional place. Identify the people's titles and the author's own title. Make a more informative subject title.

There is now a job stream available to access data element 016 in the Alumni File. The job number is S222P, and it can be found in the file cabinet by the stockroom door.

COMMENT
Begin the first sentence with something other than the weak opening—"There is."
    What will happen to this instruction if the file cabinets are ever moved?
    What is the "data element 016"?
    The pronoun "it" does not have a correct antecedent. As is, "it" modifies "number," but that is not correct. It should stand for "job stream." It is too far away from its antecedent.

Previously, only the alumni's employer code number in 016 was accessible. By using the S222P job stream, the actual name of the company can be obtained.

COMMENT
No new paragraph is needed. Information that is alike should be grouped together. Put everything about 016 together and everything about S222P together.

Although S222P requires a longer execution time, it will save at least 10 times this amount of time for the Alumni Department. They will no longer have to manually look up the company name according to the employer code number.

COMMENT
What is the basis for "10 times"? How much "longer" will the S222P require?
    "They" is plural; its antecedent, "Alumni Department" is singular. Furthermore, a department does not look things up, people do.
    Do not split the infinitive="to look up." (An *infinitive* is to plus a verb.) Say either "to look up manually" or "manually have to look up."
    "Company" and "employer" should be possessive: company's and employer's.

This new job stream will be implemented December 9, 1981 after a briefing in my office at 1 P.M. Please contact me if you can not attend.

COMMENT
Put a comma after the year.
    Where is your office? How should I contact you? Is there a phone number?
    "Cannot" is one word.
    Write the hour out in full.
    Were any copies sent? To whom?

Rewrite of Example 108
This rewrite addresses the problems and suggestions of the comments in the original example.

MEMORANDUM

TO: Dr. John Smith, Director of Computer Center
     Ms. Jane Shaw, Coordinator of Computer Center Operations
FROM: Jane Doe, Student Programmer
SUBJECT: New Way to Access Data Element 016 in Alumni File
DATE: December 8, 1981

Previously when the Alumni Department requested the name of the employer of an alumni, only the employer's code number in 016 was accessible. The job stream S222P is now available to provide more useful information. S222P has the following advantages:
1) The actual name of the company can be obtained instead of just the code number.
2) It is a cost-effective measure for the Alumni Department. Personnel will no longer manually have to search the company's name according to employer's code number.

This new job stream will be implemented after a briefing in Room A227 at 1:00 P.M. on December 18, 1981. Please contact me at 479-1234 by December 16, 1981, if you cannot attend.

copies:

Jane Adams, Director of Alumni Department

Example 109

Use the information given to write a memorandum proposing an automated process to improve this situation. Two examples follow showing results of the same assignment. Each shows an edited first draft and a clean copy.

    You are in the DP Department of ABC Company. ABC has been giving employees a cost-of-living-based salary increase for several years.
    The procedure for determining and granting increases has been:

11 MEMORANDA, STATUS REPORTS, MINUTES, SUMMARIES

1. ABC waits until all competitors announce cost of living increases, then it adjusts its own increase to fall near the average of competitors.
2. The management team reviews the salary and wage situation for every job title, compares the current salary with that of competition, then assigns a percentage increase for each job title at ABC. The Board meets to approve the management team's recommendations.
3. The Payroll and Personnel Department manually updates every eligible employee's salary by the assigned percentage then sends the new salaries to DP for keypunching and file updating, so that files will contain new salary at next payroll time.
4. Time is important. Because of the policy in item 1, employees know that other people in similar occupations in the area have already received raises; they grow impatient waiting for ABC to announce. So ABC asks for an extraordinary effort on the part of its Payroll and Personnel Department for about two weeks. In addition, temporary personnel are hired to help with clerical details such as calculating new salaries and sending a letter to each employee notifying him or her of the new salary.

Example 109A. Edited version

```
                         MEMORANDUM

TO: Curt Smith, Supervisor

FROM: Systems Analyst Group
                t   Add names
DATE: Sep/ember 16, 1983
                              ?                          precise?
SUBJECT: Proposal to Increase Automation of Salary Raise

          Process

   Add Heading:
                                   compares
       Pres/ntly, the management team reviews the current salary
                  each
       for every job title a/d comp/res /t with that of competition/
 and then assigns
  /A percentage increase per job title. is then assigned. Each em-
                         then    calculated           the employee's
       ployee's salary is /manually up/ated, keypunched, and /& file
```

is updated ~~done~~. This process requires the hiring of temporary employees and takes two weeks to complete.

Add Heading: procedure

The process can more efficiently be accomplished by the following:

② ~~reverse~~ 1. Development of a program to update each employee's salary by the required percentage.

① 2. Development of a program producing a summary report for the management team, containing salary range and average salary per job title.

3. Utilization of the word processing capabilities of the computer to produce the letters of raise notification.

Benefits:

1. Time savings—eliminates manual updating of salaries and *reduces* ~~eliminates~~ keypunching.

2. Cost savings—eliminates need to hire temporary help.

3. Employee satisfaction—*eliminates delay of raise notification* ~~salary raises are given sooner~~.

Example 109B, Rewrite, clean copy.

MEMORANDUM

TO: Curt Smith, Supervisor
FROM: System Analyst Group:
    Ed Adams, Senior Systems Analyst
    Holly Black, Systems Analyst
    Sheila Conway, Systems Analyst
    Valerie Dark, Programmer/Analyst
DATE: September 16, 1983
SUBJECT: Proposal for Additional Automation of Cost-of-Living Salary Increase Procedure

Background:

The management team compares the current salary for each job title with that of competition and then assigns a percentage increase per job title. Each employee's salary is then manually calculated and keypunched, and the employee's file is updated. This process requires the hiring of temporary employees and takes two weeks to complete.

Proposal:

The procedure can more efficiently be accomplished by the following:
1. Develop a program producing a summary report for the management team, containing salary range and average salary per job title.
2. Develop a program to update each employee's salary by the required percentage.
3. Utilize the word processing capabilities of the computer to produce the letters of raise notification.

Benefits:
1. Time savings—eliminates manual updating of salaries and reduces keypunching
2. Cost savings—eliminates need to hire temporary help
3. Employee satisfaction—eliminates delay of raise notification

PART FIVE INFORMAL WRITINGS

Example 109C. Edited version

MEMORANDUM

TO: Curt Smith, Supervisor

FROM: Data Processing Senior Group: *Add names and titles*

DATE: September 16, 1983

SUBJECT: Salary Increase Procedures) *Make more precise*

~~We feel that~~ The steps outlined below ~~could~~ would improve the current salary increase procedure and would result in ~~many~~ company and employee benefits.

1. *Develop* ~~A~~ program application ~~should be~~ developed to determine the average cost-of-living-based salary increase.

2. Creat~~ion~~e ~~of~~ an employee job file and maint~~en~~ain ~~of~~ this file ~~on a computer system should be performed by the Payroll Department~~. *the payroll department's*

3. Data Processing programmers ~~should~~ Develop a program to ~~for~~ updat~~ing~~e the ABC employee file.

4. ~~Possibility of~~ Acquir~~ing~~e *or investigate?* a word processing system for distribution letters ~~(should be investigated.)~~ ?

The major benefits of this new procedure: are the elimination of redundant paperwork, elimination of wage cost due to the hiring of temporary personnel, and greater job satisfaction for ABC employees. (We are anxiously waiting for your response to our suggested improvements.) *list these*

Make a close and rewrite

Example 109D. Revision, clean copy.

```
                    MEMORANDUM

TO; CURT SMITH, SUPERVISOR
FROM: DATA PROCESSING SENIOR GROUP:

    PAUL ADAMS, SENIOR PROGRAMMER
    EUCLID BLOCK, SENIOR PROGRAMMER
    ALAN CONALLY, SENIOR PROGRAMMER
    BRENDA DUVALL, SENIOR PROGRAMMER
DATE: SEPTEMBER 16, 1983
SUBJECT: INCREASED AUTOMATION OF SALARY REVIEW PROCEDURES

THE STEPS OUTLINED BELOW WOULD IMPROVE THE CURRENT SALARY IN-
CREASE PROCEDURE AND RESULT IN COMPANY AND EMPLOYEE BENEFITS.
    1. DEVELOP A PROGRAM APPLICATIONS TO DETERMINE THE AVERAGE
       COST-OF-LIVING-BASED SALARY INCREASE.
    2. CREATE AN EMPLOYEE JOB FILE AND MAINTAIN THIS FILE IN THE
       PAYROLL DEPARTMENT'S COMPUTER SYSTEM.
    3. DEVELOP A PROGRAM TO UPDATE THE ABC EMPLOYEE FILE.
    4. INVESTIGATE THE POSSIBILITY OF ACQUIRING A WORD PROCESS-
       ING SYSTEM FOR DISTRIBUTING LETTERS.

THE BENEFITS OF THIS NEW PROCEDURE ARE THE FOLLOWING:
    1. ELIMINATION OF WAGE COST DUE TO THE HIRING OF TEMPORARY
       PERSONNEL
    2. GREATER JOB SATISFACTION FOR ABC EMPLOYEES
    3. ELIMINATION OF REDUNDANT PAPERWORK

IN ORDER TO IMPLEMENT THE PROPOSED IMPROVEMENTS DURING THE CUR-
RENT FISCAL YEAR, PLEASE RESPOND BY SEPTEMBER 20, 1983.
```

SUMMARY COMMENT
Each rewrite emphasizes the use of the standard form, the importance of format, the need to write cleanly and clearly.

Status Reports

The report's title defines its function: it tells the status of work in progress, providing information necessary for managers and supervisors to plan work, schedule personnel, revise budgets, and anticipate implementation.

STANDARD INFORMATION FOR STATUS REPORTS

Name of project
Name of writer or names of project team members
Date
Work completed
Work in progress
Work to be done
Problems/solutions
Schedule projection/revision
Budget projection/revision
Distribution list

WRITING HINTS FOR AN EFFECTIVE REPORT

Develop a form. The report is sent regularly throughout project development (weekly, bimonthly, monthly, etc.), therefore a standard form is useful. The reader will be able to read it quickly and compare progress.
Be brief. The reader only wants to know the facts.
Be precise. For the report to be useful it must be accurate and concrete.
Be courteous. Developing, scheduling, and implementing a computer system is demanding work. Keep work relations pleasant by maintaining a courteous attitude.

EXAMPLES ON STATUS REPORTS

Example 110:

Use the "standard information" list to analyze this report. Compare your judgment with my comments. If we do not agree, determine where we differ and speculate why.

STATUS REPORT: A MANUAL FOR SELECTING A MICROCOMPUTER

(1) Five of the six individual computer sections have been completed at this point in time. The sixth section, which is on Brand Name Y, is lacking in information. The problem of finding this information is slowing our progress of the manual. However, we plan to continue according to our milestones and start putting the sections together and writing the introduction this week.

(2) Unless some substantial information can be found within the next week, we will have to eliminate Brand Name Y from the manual. Even with this problem, we hope to have the manual completed and ready for customers by the scheduled date of February 4.

COMMENT

1. Everything is wrong. Standard information is not given.
2. The format is ineffective. Even if the paragraph form is used, like items should be grouped together. For example, the problem with Brand Name Y is mentioned in paragraph (1) then again in paragraph (2). The same is true for "milestones" and schedules.
3. The tone is worrisome. Why is there a problem in "finding information"? Is it something the analyst is not doing? Does the writer have the authority to "eliminate" a section? What does that do to the original agreement or objective?
4. The language needs to be more precise: "at this point in time," "milestones," the "section . . . is lacking in information." What does this language precisely mean?

Example 111

Even though the writer chooses the memorandum form for this report and thereby standardizes its format, the report is unreadable. Determine the cause of the difficulty and compare your analysis with my comments.

```
                        MEMORANDUM
TO: Academic Computer Users Committee
    Joint Committee on Long Range Planning
    Dr. Robert Smith
    Dr. William White
FROM: Susan Smart, Analyst
SUBJECT: Status Report of the Computer Center in the School of
         Business Administration
Date: January 23, 1983
```

   The Feasibility Study was submitted on January 10, 1983. The Academic Computer Users Committee approved the recommendation of creating a Satellite Center on January 16, 1983. The Satellite Center will consist of 30 STT microcomputers located in Building B. The microcomputers will be used with the mainframe through a data communications network.

The system's specification began on January 18, 1983 and is scheduled to be completed February 10, 1983. Presently the project team believes this deadline can be met. The system's requirements were completed on January 21 and the detailed system's design will be completed by January 29, 1983. Then work will begin on the test planning and procedure specifications, which will be done concurrently. The project team will then review the system's specifications and a report will be submitted to Academic Computer Users Committee for approval on February 10, 1983.

The installation of five microcomputers in the new computer center for testing and course development is scheduled to begin on August 20, 1983. Therefore the remodeling of Building B, rooms 200 and 202 must be completed by August 15, 1983. The testing is to be completed by October 1, 1983. The major installation of the equipment is scheduled to begin June 2, 1984 and to be completed by June 30, 1984. Testing and training of personnel can be completed by August 20, 1984. I would like to thank you for your cooperation and support in this project.

COMMENT

The flood of dates, reports, and schedules makes the report unreadable. The information is not grouped in a way the reader can see work done, in progress, to be done. If I were the reader, I would be irritated that I must sort these out and make sense of them.

The report is also unreadable because it has no clear purpose or audience. Why is the opening background material included? Is the reader to manage having work done on time? For example, is the reader to see that the "remodeling" is finished by August 15? Is the reader supposed to do anything? The report is confusing.

The report needs to be rewritten. Use headings; use lists or charts or a timetable; clarify responsibilities; format using white space; separate the closing "thank you."

Example 112

The following status report uses the letter form. The first draft is edited and a rewrite follows.

First Draft

ABC COMPUTER CONSULTANTS

Woodbriar and Stoop

Grayson, Kentucky 33700

January 24, 1983

Upstate Liquor

123 Front Road

Ashland, Kentucky 38210

Dear Mr. Smith:

(This is) [Weak] a progress report about the implementation of a computer assisted optical scanning system [Caps] for the three area Upstate Liquor stores. As you can see from the Feasibility Report, which was mailed to you last week, the implementation of the system seems be be a very worthwhile project. Sixty-five percent of our portion of the project has been completed. [put related ideas together]

To date, we have observed your operation to determine your needs, after which we developed a set of alternatives to fill those needs. Once these alternatives were set forth we went to various vendors to match their products with Upstate's needs. [Make easier to see and read]

We found a company that has been in business for over sixty years, Bland Cash Register (BCR). BCR has an entire line of products designed to fit your needs and they also have the experience and maintenance program to keep your cash registers working.

As of now, we are waiting to hear from you ⟨,about⟩ before ⟨what?⟩ going any further with our plans. These plans include: establishing site preparation needs, analyzing and overseeing the training provided by BCR, and defining the computer files and procedures to use those files. Although <u>it may sound</u> as if this <u>is all we are going to do</u>, our consulting service does not stop once the first product is waved across your scanner. We will continue to be in <u>constant contact</u> with you throughout your use of the system. ⟨poor tone, do not suggest a negative⟩

We have been very pleased to serve you thus far and look forward to hearing from you very soon.

Sincerely yours,

ABC Computer Consultants

COMMENT
The writer needs to tighten language and change tone. For example, do not say "it may sound as if this is all we are going to do." Do not say you will be in "constant contact" if this is not actually true. Do not say the system "seems to be a very worthwhile project." Be positive. Format so the letter is easier to read. This rewrite makes these needed improvements.

Rewrite

ABC COMPUTER CONSULTANTS

Woodbriar at Stoop
Grayson, Kentucky 33700

January 24, 1983

Upstate Liquor
123 Front Road
Ashland, Kentucky 38210

Dear Mr. Smith:

   Sixty-five percent of the overall implementation of an Optical Scanning system for the three area Upstate Liquor stores has been completed. As you can see from the Feasibility Report, which was mailed to you last week, the implementation of the system is a worthwhile project. To date, we have completed the following:
1. Observed your operation to determine your needs
2. Developed a set of alternatives
3. Gathered information from various vendors to match products with needs

As of now, we are proceeding with the following steps:
1. Establishing site preparation needs
2. Analyzing and overseeing the training provided by BCR
3. Defining the computer files and the procedures to use those files

   We have been very pleased to serve you thus far and look forward to a continued, productive relationship.

Sincerely yours,

Alice Blank, Joe Smith, Harry Black
ABC COMPUTER CONSULTANTS

Example 113

The following two status reports use effective formats, and present material so it is easy to read and use. I comment after each.

PART FIVE INFORMAL WRITINGS

Example 113A

STATUS REPORT
JANUARY 24, 1983

PROJECT NAME: Selecting a Computer System for Accounting

PROJECT TEAM MEMBERS: Bill Jones, Vice President of Finance
Joe Nolte, Manager of Marketing
Elizabeth Sims, Senior Accountant
William Paley, Manager of Accounting

ESTIMATES:	TIME	COSTS
Original Estimates	192 man/hours	$2064.00
Work Completed	70	774.00
Estimates to Complete	122	$1290.00

WORK COMPLETED: The collect information phase of the project has been completed on schedule. Work has begun on the evaluation phase.

CURRENT WORK: Work on the evaluation phase is approximately 25% completed and should be finished on schedule by January 29.

WORK LEFT: PHASE	ESTIMATED COMPLETION DATE
75% of Evaluation	Jan. 29
Prepare and Organize	Feb. 1
Write Report	Feb. 4

PROBLEMS: None

COMMENT

1. The format is simple and easy to read. The reader can quickly find information he or she needs and use it.
2. Another line of text needs to be added to the Estimates section. The reader must add 72 + 122 to see that the project will run overtime. The same is true of Costs. The writer should do this, not the reader.
3. Under Work Left, are the completion dates on schedule? If so, say so, if not, tell how they differ from the original dates.

Example 113B

MEMORANDUM

TO: Jack Lacy, Management Information System
FROM: Marcia Morris, System Design Manager
DATE: January 20, 1983
SUBJECT: Status Report for Implementation of Microfiche System

Project:
　Implementation of a Microfiche System to solve the following problems:
　　1. Shortage of physical storage for reports
　　2. Time delays resulting from additional printing
　　3. Damage to paper reports

Work Completed:
　Work began January 11, 1983; the following tasks have been completed on schedule and within budget:
　　1. User introduction
　　2. Priority development

Work in Progress:
　The purchase and installation of microfiche equipment was delayed by 4 days due to a shipping problem. The following chart shows the revised schedule. Work has begun on installing the machinery. Completion date for installation is January 28, 1983.

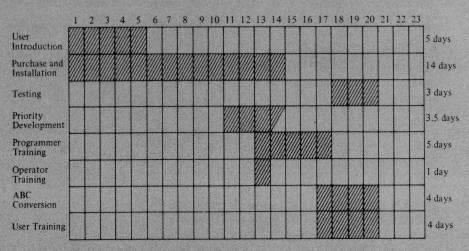

Work to Be Completed:
    Testing of system
    Training of both programmers and operators
    Conversion of ABC
    Training of users

Operators will be trained along with programmers in order to stay on schedule. ABC Conversion and User Training will begin at the same time as Programmer and Operator Training.

Schedule of Implementation Tasks:

TASKS	PERCENTAGES
Work completed	21.7
Work in progress	60.9
Work to be completed	17.4

Project Costs:
    Period ending January 24, 1983

	PROCESSOR/ DUPLICATOR	SAFE & ONE-TIME COSTS	SUPPLIES	SALES TAX
Project to date	$3,910.00	$1,800.00	$2,832.42	$324.15
Estimated cost at completion	3,910.00	1,800.00	2,832.42	259.32
Difference	0	0	0	$64.83

Cost overrun is due to 1 percent tax increase.

Date of Completion:
    February 2, 1983

Problems and Decision Needs:
    None

COMMENT
The format is effective. The information is complete and precise. The writing style is efficient. The only question is, does one need to be this elaborate? One way to decide might be to think of how many people will read this report. If several people in different positions read the report, it may need to be this complete. Another way may be to consider how often the report is sent out. If it is circulated every month, it may need to be more complete than if it is sent every week.

Minutes

Meetings are necessary to the work of system development. They take different forms—work sessions, trial runs, presentations, etc. Some but not all meetings require minutes. Since most system development teams do not have one person act as recorder for the entire project, anyone at a meeting may be asked to act as secretary. If you are asked, you need to know how to transcribe notes into an effective report of minutes.

PART FIVE INFORMAL WRITINGS

BASIC INFORMATION TO INCLUDE IN MINUTES

Meeting's name and its purpose
Called by whom
Held when and where; adjourned when
Names of those present and absent
Date of next meeting
Name of person acting as recorder
Topics discussed and summary of discussion
Copies distributed to whom

The most important writing technique to use is organization. Your task is to make order out of the discussion. If an agenda was given, you may simply list the agenda items and comment on each. At the conclusion, you can add miscellaneous subjects. If no agenda was used, you must divide the discussion into subjects and comment on each.

EXAMPLES ON MINUTES

Example 114

The following two formats serve as models for organizing.

Example 114A

```
MINUTES OF DESIGN GROUP MEETING
    August 13, 1983; 10:00 A.M. to 11:30 A.M.
    Room 113, Building X
    Those present: Al Kent, Susan Mackey, Ann Stuart, Ray
Poliakoff, Laura Stuart
    Those absent: John Calley, Alice Rider
    Acting Recorder: John Smith
    Purpose of Meeting: To Approve File Designs for Project X.


OPENING REMARKS: (SUMMARIZE)


PRESENTATION OF FILE DESIGNS FOR PROJECT X:

    (Summarize discussion; say if designs were approved or not.
If not, what is required to have them approved; why were they not
approved, or what is going to happen now?)
```

OTHER TOPICS OF DISCUSSION:

(List the topics by importance, by the order they were discussed, or by some other logical scheme. Summarize the discussion.)

DATE/TIME/PLACE OF NEXT MEETING:

Copies:

Example 114B

If the meeting is about miscellaneous subjects, you may choose to organize something like the following.

Name of meeting:
Called by whom:
Date/place/time:
Those present/absent:
Purpose:
Time and place of next meeting:
Name of recorder:

Progress Report of Project U: _____

_____

Review of Implementation Schedule for Project I: _____

_____

Report of Upcoming Projects: _____

_____

Report of Problem with Installation of SFI Computer for Project K: _____

_____

Reminder to Send Progress Reports on Time: _____

_____

SUMMARIES

Summaries are not actually "informal" reports, but because they are short and written independently after finishing any of the formal computer systems documents, they are discussed in this chapter.

Often writers will place a summary of the report between the table of contents and the introduction to the report itself. The purpose of such a summary is to highlight major information so that someone who needs only an overview of the report can read this.

A summary naturally is written last. It is impossible to write it earlier because all the facts are not known. It has become customary to place it first as a convenience for busy readers.

The summary should include an identification of the project and reasons for doing it, objectives, costs, and results. The content will vary depending upon the report but will basically tell the reader what the project is, why it was done, its costs and benefits, and what results, conclusions, and recommendations are appropriate.

The tone should be no-nonsense, clean, accurate writing.

EXAMPLES ON SUMMARIES

Example 115

The following is a good example of a summary to a system design report. It is easy to read and it tells the important points of the report.

MANAGEMENT INFORMATION SERVICES PROJECT SUMMARY

PROJECT TITLE:
Pharmaceutical Sales Call Card Analysis

PROJECT DESCRIPTION:
The purpose of this project is to analyze non-preprinted, sales call cards. The system will provide the following capabilities:

1. A means to identify the reasons why nonpreprinted call cards are used. The objective is to reduce the number submitted.
2. A means to develop reports that identify who is submitting non-preprinted call cards and what type of calls are reported. The objective is to determine if the use of non-preprinted call cards is related to the salespeople or to the type of call.

3. A means to develop a report which will tie the characteristics of physicians, such as specialty and profile rating, to the calls reported. This information will aid in determining whether representatives are making the most effective calls in accordance with the selling schedule.

JUSTIFICATION:
The new Sales Call System provides two preprinted call cards for each important physician on a representative's contact list. A representative may fill out a "non-preprinted" call card when he makes a call on a physician for whom he has no preprinted card. The company is receiving a high number of non-preprinted call cards. It needs to determine why this is occurring because of the implications in two areas:

> Significant errors in the identification of physicians can impact total Division Sales. ABCD sends preprinted call cards each selling period for approximately 155,000 physicians. The selected physicians have been identified as clients for promotion of ABCD's product. There may be inaccuracies in our physician identification procedure.

> Significant savings in manpower can be realized if the total number of non-preprinted cards can be reduced. Handling call cards in data control and keypunch is a major investment in manpower. The procedures involved in handling non-preprinted cards require a disproportionate share of the total manpower.

Estimated MIS Development Costs:
   Study (40 hrs. @ $24/hr.) $ 960.
   Design (80 hrs. @ $24/hr.)   1,920.
   Programming (160 hrs. @ $17/hr)   2,720.
   Computer Testing (12 hrs. @ $45/hr.)   540.
     TOTAL $6,140.

Estimated Annual Production Costs:
   Computer Time (5 hrs/yr. @ $45/hr.) $ 225.

Estimated Annual Savings or Contributions to Profits:
   Data Control (520 hrs. @ $14/hr.) $7,280.
   Data Services (50 hrs. @ $15/hr.)   750.
     TOTAL ANNUAL SAVINGS $8,030.

The primary benefits from this project will be realized from making the sales call effort more effective.

SCHEDULE:

	MIS Dev. Hrs	Start	Complete
Study	40	7/19/82	8/06/82
Design	80	8/09/82	8/31/82
Programming/Testing	160	9/01/82	1/31/83

General Summary

Pull out memoranda, status reports, minutes, and summaries you have written or received. Analyze their effectiveness. Determine how you will improve your own writing of these informal reports.

CHECKLIST: CHAPTER 11
Memoranda, Status Reports, Minutes, Summaries

MEMORANDA
: Allows writers to exchange information informally
  Writing Suggestions:
    Use a standard form.
    Keep to one page if possible.
    Organize information so it is easy to see. Use lists, headings, outlines, and white space.
    Type whenever possible.
    Be consistent in format and organization.
    Make headings precise.
    Identify subsequent pages by subject, date, page numbers.
    Sign only if you wish.
    Omit complimentary close.

STATUS REPORTS
: Tells the status of work in progress.
  Standard Information:
    Name of project
    Name of writer or project team members
    Date
    Work completed, in progress, to be done
    Problems/solutions
    Schedule projection/revision
    Budget projection/revision
    Distribution list
  Writing Suggestions:
    Develop a standard form.
    Be brief.
    Be precise.
    Be courteous.

MINUTES
: Records the proceedings of meetings.
  Standard Information:
    Meeting's identity and its purpose
    Called by whom
    Held when and where; adjourned when
    Names of those present and absent
    Date of next meeting
    Name of recorder
    Topics discussed and summary of discussion
    Copies distributed to whom
  Writing Suggestions:
    Organize by agenda or topics, but make order out of the discussion.

PART FIVE   INFORMAL WRITINGS

SUMMARIES   Gives an overview of the report being presented.
Standard Information:
   Project's identity and rationale
   Objectives, costs, and results
   Conclusions and recommendations
Writing Suggestions:
   Write last.
   Adopt a no-nonsense tone.
   Write clearly and accurately.
   Write about the essentials.

PART SIX

CONCLUSION

The whole of this book is an effort to help you improve your ability in applying good writing practices in writing computer system documentation and in analyzing documentation in order for you to know whether what you or others write is effective.

Now is the time to care about your ability to write and to analyze. Everywhere you look, in articles in computer magazines, course offerings for in-house training, and speech topics at computer conventions, the need for better computer system documentation is talked about. Data processors, manufacturers, clients, and users recognize the cost of poor documentation.

If you write well and can analyze the writing of others on the system documentation team and offer constructive advice, you will be respected and recognized.

Remember that system documentation is never complete. Systems are modified and every change requires a written record. Use all that you have learned in this book to design documentation that can be updated. Be as diligent and accurate about maintenance documentation as you are about the original effort.

Good writing is hard work, but it has its rewards. For a task like writing one of the system's major documents, you have the satisfaction of accepting a challenge, working through it, and completing it. You have the pleasure of making words on paper say to others exactly what you are thinking. You have the opportunity to lay out information on a page or to organize a report so that the writing mirrors the logic of your thought. You have the respect of your colleagues for being able to say what you mean in an understandable way.

I wish you the pleasure of such rewards.

Index

Active voice, 15, 97
Analogy, 214
Analysis, 4, 51, 207
Audience analysis, 10, 22, 40, 60, 67, 68, 92, 124, 248

Be responsible for what you write, 16, 60

Cause and effect, 47, 57, 61
Charts, 78–83, 123, 202, 203
Checklists
   rules to remember, 20
   structure your writing, 49
   proposal I, 56
   proposal II, 89
   functional specification I, 102
   functional specification II, 126
   system specification I, 159–160
   system specification II, 205–206
   user's manual, 234
   memoranda, status reports, minutes, summaries, 261–262
Classification and division, 26–36, 117
Comparison and contrast, 24–25, 62–63, 70, 71
   block method, 24
   point-by-point, 25
Conclusion, 263
Cover page (see Title page)
Critic, 4, 6, 9, 10, 13, 14, 55, 131

Definition, 21–24, 36, 37
Definition structures
   analogy, 22
   etymology, 22
   class and difference, 22
   analysis, 22
   characteristics, 22
   elimination, 22
   extended definition, 22
Description, 36–38
Design, 4, 127
Document analysis, 6, 22

Formal outline form, 138
Format, 14, 37, 43, 60, 62, 67, 69, 84, 96, 100, 106, 142, 168, 210, 247, 251, 253, 255, 256
Functional specification, 4, 16,
   definition and purpose, 90
   writer, 91
   reader, 91, 99

265

INDEX

good work habits, 91–92
outline
  identify report, 93
    examples, 93–95
  reintroduce idea, 95–96
    examples, 96–98
  assumptions, 98
    examples, 98–99
  glossary, 99–100
    examples, 100–101
  input/output, 103
    examples, 103–112
  responsibilities, 112
    examples, 112–118
  hardware, 118
    examples, 119–120
  data retention, 120
    examples, 120–121
  security, 121–122
    examples, 122–124
  audits, 124
    examples, 124–125

Implementation, 4, 207
Informal writings, 235
Input/output, 90, 68, 182

Look at words, 18

Manuals, 4, 10, 12, 43–47, 129, 207–208
Memoranda, 237–238
  writing suggestions, 238
    examples, 238–245
Minutes, 255–256
  examples, 256–257

Narration, 39

Outline, 12–13

Paragraphing, 63, 179, 239
Parallelism (see Structure alike)

Persuasion, 7, 48, 53,
  historical approach, 7–9
  shock approach, 9
Procedure, 43–47
Process analysis, 39–42
Program specifications, 4, 40–43
Proofread, 19
Proposal, 4, 7, 11, 12,
  definition and function, 53–54
  writer, 54
  reader, 54
  outline
    statement of problem, 23, 57–58, 96, 98
    statement of solution, 58, 96, 98
      examples, 58–67
    operational requirements, 67
    operating environment, 68
      examples, 17, 68–69
    benefits, 69
      examples, 69–75
    budget, 75
      examples, 76–78
    implementation plan, 78
      examples, 78–83
    evaluation, 83
      examples, 83–84
    alternatives, 84
      examples, 85–88

Status reports, 245–246
  writing hints, 246
    examples, 246–255
Structure alike (parallelism), 72–73, 86, 138, 193, 227
Structure your writing, 21
Summaries, 258
  examples, 258–260
System specification, 4,
  definition and function, 129
  writer, 129
  reader, 129
  good writing habits, 130–131
  outline
    identify report and contents, 131

examples, 131–134
reintroduce idea, 134
  examples, 134–142
chart system information, 142
  flowcharts, 143–144
    examples, 144–152
  data flow diagrams, 152–153
    examples, 153–158
define data, 161
  data dictionaries, 161–162
    examples, 162–164
  files, records, and fields, 164–165
    examples, 166–178
  processing controls, 178
    examples, 178–181
  program narratives, 182
    examples, 182–187
  operating characteristics, 188
    examples, 188–191
  restrictions and trade-offs, 191
    examples, 191–197
  costs and schedules, 197
    examples, 197–203
  system test plan, 203

Tables, 112–114
Table of contents, 13, 93, 132–135, 212
Talkthrough, 55
Tense, 72, 97
Title page, 93, 131–135, 211
Tone, 11, 12, 71, 72, 141, 213, 247, 250, 258

Updating procedures, 4
User's manual
  definition and function, 209
  writer, 209
  reader, 209
  good writing habits, 209–210
  writing suggestions, 210–211
  outline
    introduction, 211
      examples, 211–217
    instructions, 217
      examples, 43–47, 217–233

Walkthrough, 55
Writing rules to remember, 6

Notes

Notes

Notes